TIME SPACE AND DRUMS SUPPLEMENT

MODERN DRUMMING CONCEPTS

TIME SPACE AND DRUMS SUPPLEMENT

MODERN DRUMMING CONCEPTS

A Beginners Guide to Drumming Practice & Development

The Time Space & Drums Series
A Complete Program of Lessons in Professional, Contemporary Rock, and Jazz Drumming Styles.

Written and Developed By:
Stephen Hawkins

Graphic Design By: Nathaniel Dasco.
Special Thanks To Linda Drouin and Ikhide Oshoma

ThinkeLife Publications

Time Space and Drums Copyright 2018 By Stephen Hawkins.

All Rights Reserved.

No part of this book may be reproduced in any form or by any electronic or mechanical means including information storage and retrieval means without permission in writing from the author.

The only exception is by a reviewer, who may quote short excerpts in a review.

Stephen Hawkins - Time Space and Drums
Visit my website at www.timespaceanddrums.com

First printing: Jan 2018.

ISBN: 978 1 913929 12 1

Dedicated to the late Paul Daniels and family, Martin Daniels, Trevor Daniels, Paul Mellor's, Keith Richards, Chris Moreno, Peter Windle, Andrew Marple's, Colin Keys, Peters & Lee, Susan Maughan, Ronnie Dukes, Tom O'Connor, Les Dennis, Bob Monkhouse, Bobby Davro, Tommy Bruce, Robert Young, Sandie Gold as well as the hundreds of other people who have played a part in my life experience. Including Sphinx Entertainment, E & B Productions as well as the hundreds of fantastic personalities I have had the pleasure of working alongside over the past 35 years. Apologies for anyone I have missed, not forgetting the current reader who I hope will receive as much from their drumming as I have and more – Stephen Hawkins.

Table of Contents

Section 1 1

    INTRODUCTION 2
        Finding the Right Teacher For YOU! 3
    The Division. 3
    Your First Step is to find answers to these questions. 4
    LOCAL TEACHERS 5
        Foundations for YOUR Success! 6
    So, what makes up a good foundation? 7
    An Example 8
        YOUR Roadmap to Wealth! 8
    More Than Just A Drummer! 9
    The First Steps on Your Journey 9
        REGULAR PRACTICE! 10
    THE STRUCTURE. 11

Section 2 12

    POSTURE! 13
    Hand Positions! 14
    ARE THERE ANY DIFFERENCES BETWEEN MATCHED AND TRADITIONAL GRIP? 14
    Balance Points 15
        Foot Positions! 15
        BALANCE! 16
        Mind Over Body! 18
        The Science and Art of Drumming! 19
        From the Beginning to The End and Back! 20
    THE BEGINNING 21

Section 3 22

        Your First Kit 23
    Basic Needs and Requirement! 23
    Basic Necessities 23
        Quality Sound! 25
    DRUM TUNING! 25

FELT BEATERS 25
NYLON TIPS 26
Strike Up the Beat - OR NOT? 26
The Point 26
Looking ahead to Your Uniqueness! 27
Don't Forget the Fun! 27
Sound Quality 28
    Built to Last & Room for Development 29
    Long Practice? Silent Practice 30
Lower the Decibels 30
    Playing for Fun - Playing Vs Practice 31
Practice Versus Playing 32
    Roadmap to Success! 33
The First Step in The Right Direction 33

Section 4 34

    Beginner Tips 35
FRESH AIR, the Greatest Value to Human Life & Drummers. 35
THE BIG PICTURE 36
    Bringing Inner Understanding into Solid Reality. 37
JUST STICKS! 37
    More Improvement Tips 39
PRACTICE PADS 39
The Goal is ACCURACY NOT SPEED. 40
The Feet 41
ADDING THE BASS DRUM PRACTICE 41
ADD HI-HAT Pedal ON left Foot 42
    TURN THOSE DRUMS DOWN! 42
THE LAST RESORT or Is It? 43
AIR PLAYING 43
SUBCONSCIOUS IGNORANCE 43
The Theory of Practice - The Theory behind the Theory - 4 Stages of Learning 44
PLAYING DRUMS IS EASY 44
What do I mean by perfect? 44
WHEN IS THE BEST TIME TO BEGIN LEARNING DRUMS? 45
A COMMON MISCONCEPTION 46
    So, Let's Talk About Me 46
Intermediate Drummer Tips 48
Advanced Techniques 49
What You Play and Where You Play It. 51
Time Does Not Exist 52
Measuring Time 53

The Point 55
Original Title 55
Closing Note: 56
Afterword 56

Section 1

Taking Your First Steps

INTRODUCTION

Although it is intended to be supplemental to the Time Space and Drums series this book also serves as an introduction or getting started manual for the complete beginner and possibly the intermediate drummer. The first section being specifically for the complete beginner and the second section aimed at the intermediate to the advanced drummer in an attempt to add some modern concepts to his or her existing arsenal of drumming skills and abilities.

The more advanced drummers may find some new ideas and concepts throughout the second section of this short book and possibly the first section that helps him or her advance even further or at the very least get even more control over one's current skills and abilities.

The astute reader will understand that even the most basic ideas could add a little or a lot to one's current abilities through digging the neural pathways a little deeper and therefore even the first section of this book could be of potential value to higher level drummers.

I will leave it up to the individual reader to make up their own minds regarding such judgments and hope that even if I make a little impact on just one student of drums then my work will have been worth the effort. I know of no greater reward than a glint of discovery in a student's eye!

But as you will discover, in general, I tend to listen to the beat of a different drummer, always have, and that has kept me living on the edge of life just a little. I think it's smart to keep a honed focus and not to let others diffuse your efforts whatever road you decide to travel. As drummers, we tend to express our individualism in one way or another regardless of others' opinions unless it serves us to do so anyway, and that's a good thing. We don't want to waste our valuable time by creating anything less than what is good for us and the music we play.

And speaking of wasting our time, although some videos can be entertaining and others can be useful tools to learn from I believe the written word carries more weight in the readers' mind as the synapses start to fire as we dig those neural pathways just a little deeper than when we are passively watching TV or videos. Reading is a more active way of learning so I believe it to have more value than videos despite the recent years' video site eruptions into our lives.

Due to its passive nature, I try to avoid extended viewing times much like the TV as I am far too busy developing my own projects and life to sit watching others live theirs. But that is just my wayward opinion and me exerting my own influence into my own life and the path I choose to follow. You may be different and that is fine too.

Having said that, don't spend too much time watching other people live their lives to the extent that your own rushes by you in an attempt to avoid those long hard practice sessions needed to make it in the world of drumming today.

Don't let anyone tell you any different. Drumming can be a long and often frustrating path to take if you intend playing professionally on one level or another in the not so distant future.

But for now, let's take our first steps into the various drumming concepts the drummer will need to make use of whether they be tangible or intangibly attained as he travels down the road to drumming control and mastery.

Finding the Right Teacher For YOU!

Let's start with some beginning steps you will have to take at the onset of your drumming career. More advanced drummers can also benefit from spending more time on their basic fundamental knowledge, skills, and abilities and so I make no apology for inviting more advanced players to read this first section as well as the more advanced concepts in section two of this little book. As touched upon in the introduction, everything can always be made better and those neural pathways can always be ground a little or indeed much deeper.

So, you need a drum teacher, instructor, or guide? First, let's begin by summing up exactly what a teacher is and what he is not.

A drum teacher is someone who teaches you "the right way" to learn how to play the drums. In this, he is really a guide and not a teacher at all.

This is because within your own mind you always teach yourself and are only guided by the external influence of the teacher. You see, hear and find errors you are making within yourself based on the guidance provided of what is the right or best way to learn from that particular teacher's perspective and you decide to correct those errors or not.

This Division.

Although you are your own teacher for the time being let me take on that role and you can take over when the time is right for you. The most important part of being a drum guide or instructor as we'll call him is, in the beginning at least, is possessing some knowledge and or skill that you/the student/teacher wish to learn. In order to know this, you must first know where you want to go as a drummer and within the world of drumming.

Do you just want to play for fun or do you want to play in a band? If the later, what kind of band? What kind of music would they play? what kind of gigs would they do?

Do you want to master all styles of drumming or just concentrate your efforts on rock or jazz or any other musical style? I should clarify from the onset that whether you want to learn reggae, blues, jazz, rock, Latin bebop, rap, or any other kind of music genre that in drumming these two distinctions (rock and jazz) should really be made clear. Drumming is drumming and as a member of the rhythm section in a band situation what you are doing as a drummer falls into two main categories. In its most basic form, these categories might be called straight ahead 1/8th notes and triplets. Or rock and jazz.

All music genres or styles as far as drumming is concerned are formed from the foundations of those two drumming rhythms, rock and jazz. If you want to be a rock drummer you learn rock and jazz drumming, if you want to be a jazz drummer you learn jazz and rock drumming and if you want to be any other kind of drummer you learn rock and jazz drumming.

So, you now understand the foundations of drumming but those two rhythms are built on the foundation of the quarter note, pulse, or time. Both jazz and rock rhythms are built on the ¼ note pulse and so the two drumming rhythms rock and jazz although written differently are really just different feels built on the foundation of the pulse. They describe how the drumming or music feels and so are written differently in order to express those two feels of jazz and rock or swing and rock. Swing is essentially the same as jazz.

If there is anything you don't understand from the above description then reread this section as it is an important foundational concept that all drummers must integrate and master so don't be put off by the terms jazz and rock if you want to be a pop or R&B drummer, for instance, jazz and rock styles will take you there. But remember that both jazz and rock are built on the foundation of the ¼ note or pulse of the music so the pulse is divided into two feels or styles of drumming.

Your First Step is to find answers to these questions.

Before we made the distinction between the two styles of drumming, we were thinking about what we want from our drumming? So, do you just want to play for fun or do you want to play in a band? If the later, what kind of band? What kind of music would they play? what kind of gigs would they play on?

When you have the answers to these questions only then can you find the right teacher for you, which makes perfect sense? However, if you have already had some experience and learned the basic jazz and rock rhythms then you may indeed want to find a teacher who specializes in a particular style or genre of music. That said, a good teacher will know all styles anyway at least a little so it is a question of how far can you get with a particular teacher?

And so, if you want to specialize in rock drumming you can search for and find a teacher who specializes in rock drumming. It's that simple but bear in mind that jazz and rock styles or rhythms work hand in hand so to speak.

However, as previously iterated it is important at the beginning to understand that there are core skills you must learn to be good at any style of drumming. In this, choosing a particular style is a secondary decision usually made a couple of years into your drumming studies when you have built a good solid foundation. Then there's the fact that most good teachers would be able to set you on the road towards a particular drumming style or genre anyway.

You can take the road of least resistance if you wish, meaning that you learn to play the drums and decide where you want to go from that vantage point, knowing your strengths and weaknesses in a particular area that you have developed if any.

With all of the previous conclusions in mind, you need to decide exactly what it is you want to achieve? If you don't know where you want to go you will find it very difficult to get there?

It's a good idea to write your ideas down at the beginning just to keep you on track. And it's a good idea to keep some kind of journal or record-keeping system so that you can develop your needs and requirements, ideas, goals, and aspirations as you progress.

To begin, answer these questions and find other questions and answer them according to your likes and dislikes.

- **What kind of music do you like to listen to?**
- **What kind of bands do you like to listen to?**
- **Who is your favorite drummer?**
- **Who are your top 10 favorite drummers?**
- **What do you want to achieve from your drumming?**
- **Do you want to be famous?**
- **Do you want to just be a fantastic drummer?**
- **Do you want to travel? If so where to? How far?**

In short, list anything that describes you and what you want to achieve from music and drumming. Get your goals and aspirations clear and make them clear on paper so that you know where your heading.

Ok, so some of these questions may seem irrelevant at the moment and so you may like to make a note of them in a notebook and answer them later. Revise your questions often and add questions to the list as you think of them. The clearer you are about your goals the more directly and easily you will achieve them.

The most valuable thing you can do at the beginning of a drumming career is to ask questions. Ask other drummers, ask your local drum store, ask anyone who may be able to help you find the right answers in order to refine your direction. And of course, lead you to more questions that need answering?

Stanford University did a lot of research in goal setting and found that the ones who set goals whilst still at school were the highest achievers after 20 years or so. They knew where they wanted to go and so setting goals made them more likely to get there?

LOCAL TEACHERS

Then you can begin by making a list of drum instructors in your local area and call them. Find out the cost of lessons and how long you would need them as a complete beginner or whatever level you are currently at? what do they specialize in? Ask these and other questions in order to make an intelligent informed decision on the direction you would like to take in the future and the drum teacher you decide to go with.

Don't get pushed into taking lessons from someone until you have collected your information. Then if you find a suitable instructor, book a lesson and take it from there.

The Time Space and Drums Series is designed for all drummers just starting out and contains the core skills and others you will need to know whatever style you decide to specialize in if any. This is why the series is suitable to study and practice alongside any outside tutor. It will only enhance your drum instructors' teachings.

Remember the Time Space and Drums Series was designed to be studied and practiced at the very beginning of your drumming career but I believe all basic knowledge is suitable for all drummers of all levels, even if they just learn some basic concepts and ways of thinking about their drumming.

At the very least you should book a lesson so you can learn how to hold the drumsticks, how best to sit and play your foot pedals and so on. Once these basic concepts have been grasped you can take a course such as the Time Space and Drums Series without any teacher whatsoever. I say this confidently because a good part of your drum practice should be all about the theory of drum music and playing what is written exactly. This is how the Time Space & Drums series was developed, as a step by step process that teaches the non-reading drummer to learn to read drum music and play drums at the same time.

Foundations for YOUR Success!

Whatever style of drumming you decide to specialize in, whatever instructor you decide to employ, you need to make sure that you have a fantastically solid rock foundation of drumming skills. This is the first priority.

You cannot build a great and mighty structure without any foundations! Plain and Simple.

The Time Space and Drums Series contain all of the theoretical and foundation skills necessary to build a great knowledge base to begin building your drumming foundational skills. As mentioned, it's a great tool to run alongside any drum tuition methods even if some of those methods are more advanced than the Time Space and Drums Series. Whilst you learn from a drum instructor you are also laying a solid foundation to build on later.

Again, whether you use a teacher or various books to develop your skills and there are literally hundreds of books to choose from and I recommend a variety of drum books in order to learn from different drummers and the variety of different perspectives and methods they use. In the end, the methods will all integrate to make the student a much better and diversified player and not just a rock drummer, or jazz drummer or pop drummer, and so on.

So, what makes up a good foundation?

I'll explain in more detail within the series but basically, a good understanding of the following is essential to your drumming foundation. I will include a brief reason why.

1 - Knowledge of at Least One Great Drummer. Without knowing the skill of the competition how can you hope to emulate or even better them? This again all ties in with setting goals with your own drumming and remember this, I use the term competition very loosely as all drummers have something to offer to another drummer without any rivalry or antagonistic points of view entering the mix.

2 - Drum Kits Available. You need to make the very best of what you can afford and to do this you need to know what's available to you and the cost involved.

3 - Music Theory - In particular Drum Notation and Time Signatures. This helps you to learn specific exercises you may see or hear later both within the Time Space and Drums Series as well as other drumming resources. You are then more easily able to play and interpret songs that you need to learn by writing drum guides for songs. I have made a free Glossary of Musical Terms available at timespaceanddrums.com.

4 - Drum Rudiments - Without learning the letters of the language of drums you cannot understand the words or rhythms of drumming. You can only speak a language you have learned from the ground up and drumming is one such language. You might call rudiments the core skills of all drumming, they are the letters that you use to string words and sentences (beats and rhythms) together. The better they become the more easily and better everything else in your playing gets.

5 - Various Rhythms and Beats — Foundation Rock, Jazz, Latin style rhythms and beats in order to play a variety of music styles beginning from and then building on those initial roots. These work hand in hand with the rudiments.

6 - Various Drumming Concepts - 2 against 3, 5's, 7's, and 9 Groupings. Playing backward, poly-rhythms, Floating Around the Kit, and others. These add creativity to your foundation skills making for a more advanced foundation. Remember I say advanced foundation because you are always at the very beginning and making the fundamentals better. As a beginner, you would be concerned with learning the basic beats and as an intermediate to an advanced player, you would be concerned with playing those same beats better.

7 - Tuning setup and other basic techniques.

The above foundation skills along with a few others you may bump into that are mostly individualistic give you the full understanding of your instrument and allowing for better execution of your skills later.

These basic techniques are advanced to the degree of mastery by the drummer.

This is the journey I like to call FROM THE BEGINNING TO THE END AND BACK. Or Advanced Techniques are just Basic Techniques – MASTERED or played MASTERFULLY.

An Example

Imagine if you will a tall skyscraper or multi-storeyed hotel. Probably the most important part of that structure is the foundation as, without it, the building just wouldn't exist, and if it did exist it wouldn't stand for very long.

Have you ever watched a building being constructed? beginning from a flat piece of spare land? well, nothing gets done for weeks or so it appears. Actually, the foundation is dug downward, a concrete foundation laid, water pipes and drains laid, supplies of water, electricity, etc. are prepared. All of these foundational requirements are set in place ready for the structure to be built later.

Then all of a sudden, the building starts to grow outward and upward at an incredible rate.

The next day the building appears to have doubled in size, and the next day and the next until all of a sudden, the structure is built. All the structure needs now are the refining touches, cleaning up, or decorating so to speak.

When the foundation is solid The Structure Grows Rapidly.

Tiles on the roof, window frames, glass, drain pipes, electricity, plaster on the walls, light switches, a bath, sink, tiles, etc. Until the finishing coat of paint and or wallpaper is added.

All of which cannot be started until a solid Rock Foundation is built and the structure is erected.

This is the first goal of any drummer, to Build a fantastically solid Rock Drumming Foundation!

YOUR Roadmap to Wealth!

Wealth can be defined as a large quantity of, means, assets, material possessions.

You cannot become a great drummer without first accumulating a large number of assets. This simply means that you need to gather the materials required, which are "drumming concepts and skills" more aptly foundation skills, in order to increase the quality of those assets to again make them great assets later and as you progress towards your goals.

When I first developed the series of books, I envisioned that the 12 books were a 12-month program, then looking deeper realized that the complete beginner would most likely require approximately 6 weeks per book to really get the exercises. Then it came to me that maybe any level student should take the 4 - 6 weeks and work on each part of the series then do the same again for the following 12 months. Left hand lead if the student was after a challenge.

After which it should be relatively simple to repeat the whole process again over 12 weeks (one book per week) once or twice before going through the whole series in 12 days, at which point the focus would most likely change from one of building a foundation to developing the structure.

In all of this, it is clear that wealth of this kind is really a self-created decision to build that which is required as an end result. Ours being a wealth of drumming skills and theoretical information or a solid foundation.

Here I am not simply referring to drumming skills as such, for what good is being a fantastic drummer if you don't have the superb health to travel to the gig, set the kit up and play the drums all night long which requires some stamina and good health and fitness in the first place.

In short, it is not just drumming skills we require in order to become great. We need to increase our intelligence, our health, relationships, and other aspects of our life and being in order to become a well-rounded individual first and then drummer.

More Than Just A Drummer!

For this reason, we will be making available a variety of subjects to the drum student in order for him/her to increase his knowledge of his art and himself including goals, self-belief, attitude, and more. These will all become available within and through the Time Space and Drums Series.

However, drumming is our main concern here so don't think I'm going totally off track. I am just illustrating the need to become aware and concerned with more than our drumming skills at the beginning of the journey – if that journey is to become as fruitful as possible.

The First Steps on Your Journey

Of course, we must view ourselves at the beginning in order to start along the road and increase our wealth of any kind and as they say, all journeys start with the first step or steps.

In the beginning, we must prepare and plan our route or at the very least have an approximation of the result we are seeking, and to do this our timekeeping must be impeccable not just on the drum kit but off the drum kit also. We become a business person. Our business in this instance is becoming a great drummer and that involves timing and scheduling everything that we do in order to make sure we get there.

Our arrival point will be much sweeter depending on the scheduling, tasks, and projects completed and mastered by the time that arrival point comes. They say that success is when preparedness meets opportunity and so if that is true then we owe it to ourselves to make the best preparations we are capable of and more, if possible.

Which of course brings up the arrival point.

How long will it take you to get there? Make an estimate and refine it as you go based on your ability to learn and practice. Jot down answers and questions in your notebook and keep refining your vision in order to better clarify your arrival point and where exactly you will be arriving. The Stanford study I mentioned earlier showed that the most successful people in the world are the ones who make setting goals a priority. Even if it's just a set of songs you need or want to learn. We then begin to control our lives rather than being controlled by it or reacting to what happens to us.

Create benchmarks to be reached along the way, at which time, by all means, celebrate but don't become complacent. Reward yourself yes, but remember to set more goals along the way then clarify them along with your hopes and dreams in order to increase your wealth of both knowledge and skill in drumming and life.

Make your life a learning, study, practice, and wisdom gathering experience and the effect of such knowledge and skill will be one of success and wealth personally as well as financially.

Or something like that. This is all a case of working on the cause to affect a good or better effect.

It is said that to earn more you must learn more but that doesn't mean just money. Start learning now in order to earn more respect and recognition later, when you have gathered the skills required of you which is totally dependent on your goal in the first place. So, start planning and preparing now for the first or next big drumming job.

REGULAR PRACTICE!

Let's face it, you get a drumming job in the first place because you practiced a lot, right? and that's exactly how you keep the job, by practicing **a lot** more.

It's not enough these days to get the gig then become complacent. You need continued, planned, practice, and development. Practice both the music you're playing as well as your own development and technique.

Your development should be divided into parts that will all need work and effort to produce even better results in the future.

First your rudiments - then your kit sound - your jazz style - your rock style - Latin styles and others - your health and fitness - stamina and energy - improved memory and concentration - confidence and attitude as well as goals and time management techniques. All of these are important in life and drumming. You must take advantage of each to become the best you can be at what you do and what is possible for you and your life.

From here you really leave the drumming world and enter the self-improvement world. In short - you need to work on the functionality of the drummer as well as the drumming. The engine that drives the car so to speak, must be well oiled and serviced. And if you don't control the things that I just mentioned you are controlled by them for better or worse.

As you develop yourself your drumming will improve systematically. You'll begin to put more into your art by developing the science of what you're doing to a much deeper level.

The Time Space and Drums Series includes this development process integrally. It's an evolution into something more than the foundation but as a beginner, you should concentrate on the foundation for a while. Perhaps something close to erm… a lifetime? But this is fun, isn't it? If it wasn't why do it in the first place?

THE STRUCTURE.

The structure must be as solid as the foundation itself. Indeed, it is the foundation. Only then can you really add the finesse or decor? You clean everything up which basically means you improve the quality of everything that you do. Beginning and returning to the basic fundamentals. From the beginning to the end and back again, and again… well, you get the picture.

You improve your playing to the degree that the time becomes solid and tight. Then space becomes clean space that will help other musicians want to work with you more and more.

Section 2

The Drummer

POSTURE!

Beginning here again with the drummer in mind, good posture is everything.

From a practical point of view, the first thing that the drummer needs to consider before you begin to play the drums is your seating position or posture. Despite the long hours you will most likely spend sat at your drum set, with the correct posture you not only feel better you actually play better.

Using correct posture can relieve depression, stress, avoid back neck and shoulder pain and tension, and can have other benefits including improved spinal alignment and breathing to name a few.

To begin thinking about the general posture you simply need to become aware of your back, its position, and alignment. Keep it erect with your chin up and horizontal to the ground and if at all possible, avoid moving your body too much when a simple head movement or turn to the side will do the trick.

In your daily life don't bend or slouch to pick up items if all that is required is for you to move your arm or bend your legs a little to pick the item up? Sounds simple I know, but a lot of people bend their back to pick up an item that is within arm's reach and requires no back bending at all.

I am by no means an expert in this department but it serves the drummer to instead of just do or perform an act to instead think about the way in which he performs that act as he performs it to make sure his body doesn't suffer through creating bad habits of movement and lifting etc, as well as sitting at the drum set.

As a drummer, sit at your kit with your back straight on a comfortable sturdy stool. Place both feet flat on your pedals then lift your heel about 1-2 inches from the pedalboard. Hover your hands over the kit so that you play with everything within easy reach or striking distance including cymbals as well as drums.

Always try to keep your back and neck straight.

I urge you now to do yourself a favor and buy yourself a book called Beat Back Pain with the Alexander Technique: Teach Yourself or any book on this subject for that matter and make this posture technique a valuable part of your drumming development.

Using this technique doesn't require you to have back pains. The purpose of practicing this posture technique is to avoid back problems in the future and to increase your focus and skill as a drummer now.

More aptly this back and movement technique is all about re-education. We all need to re-educate ourselves and our bodies to the true body's positions, movements, and alignment.

Who didn't develop bad habits in the past? Slouching and bending the body over a desk at school for instance. Add this technique to your drumming and life in order to be absolutely sure you never suffer from back problems later, and that you receive the benefits of the technique now such as increased focus and concentration which are among the drummers most valuable assets should he desire to improve beyond the beginner to intermediate level.

This is about providing the best value and knowledge and placing it before you so you can benefit from my own experiences. If you feel unsure you can ask your doctor about the benefits of the Alexander Technique. I will from time to time recommend specific books that Time Space and Drums do make a very small commission from but I add the recommendations to add value as I just mentioned and not to make money.

Hand Positions!

The next subject we should mention as drummers are the position of your hands and arms. Thinking of hand positions brings to mind the kit in general and as suggested in the previous section. In short, don't have the kit set up with your cymbals so far away that you have to bend your back, neck, or body to reach out, over, or up to them.

Try to avoid having them either too high or too low that you either have to bend your back and neck to look down at them or have your neck bent looking up towards them. In short, position your cymbals and drum kit at hand height and within a stick and arms distance with your whole body sat erect in the core seating position as previously discussed. This will leave your mind to focus on the important stuff of playing the drums and thus you won't be spending valuable energy trying to find the cymbals above you?

Once the kit is positioned correctly you can begin to focus on your hands.

I have used the matched grip style for over 30 years and have only recently begun to practice traditional grip. This has caused many problems for me including:

1. My left wrist and arm have proven too weak to play consistently as I used to do. I have virtually no left-hand strength or power now.

2. My left-hand matched grip seems to be getting worse. This is probably not true and instead, it just feels a little awkward due to the effort I'm putting into learning the traditional grip style. I have a long way to go with that still.

Of course, both problems can be remedied after I begin gaining power in my left hand and wrist again but that will take time. Itis coming together slowly but is still far from being up to scratch.

ARE THERE ANY DIFFERENCES BETWEEN MATCHED AND TRADITIONAL GRIP?

Regarding the different stick positions, I have seen and heard other drummers answering the question which is the best position to hold the sticks traditional or matched grip and most say that there are basically no differences. One drummer does admit that he plays the traditional grip for looser style playing and music and uses a matched grip when the music requires him to play more powerfully.

However, the drummer I am speaking of has more than likely been playing traditional grip for a long time and probably played matched grip also. Being experienced at both styles to a high degree would probably mean there are few practical differences.

However, that said, I did find that as I get more control over the left-hand grip I seem to be playing more creatively. This is most likely due to the fact that the experts say the right side of the brain is responsible for more creative acts and its supposed function is to control the left side of the body. The Left side of the brains' supposed function is related to analytical thinking processes and controls the right side of the body. If you want to look deeper into that here is a good place to start http://bit.ly/2Sv6Lhg.

Balance Points

I have described how to hold the drum sticks fully in the Rock Drumming Foundation book as well as the accompanying Modern Drumming Concepts Videos and so will just touch on it again here. If you just drop the stick on the drum it will simply bounce off of the head a few times but if you try to control that bounce you can hit the drum then by clasping the drumstick slightly by making the following movements and positions holding the sticks becomes a simple matter that can develop further over time. It is that bounce that you are going to learn to control. The entire movement of the stick repeated over and over again would look something like this.

Stick up, stick halfway down, stick on the drum, stick bounce off again, stick halfway up, then repeat the process. See the accompanying video for a clear demonstration of how to hold the sticks and this basic stick movement.

Foot Positions!

After the drummer has successfully attained a good healthy posture the feet positions are easily assimilated.

First, gain your seating position then place both feet flat on the pedalboards then when you have done this and checked your posture again to make sure your spine is fully aligned. You should then lift both of your heels an inch or so off of the pedalboards.

Your bass drum pedal beater will be against the drum head at this point and your hi-hat cymbals will be closed but loosely.

Move your toes so that they are approximately one third the way down the pedalboard (approx. 2 inches each). Both feet.

This is the basic start position.

Now lift the whole of your right leg without taking the front of your foot off of the pedalboard. This will move the beater away from the drum head as you lift. Then slightly before the beater is fully pulled back release and press the pedal with your right foot. Not too hard, just strike the drum with the beater by pressing your foot down.

At this point don't just leave the beater pressed into the drum head. Remove it straight away by slightly lifting your knees/whole leg off of the pedal but never removing the front of the foot off of the pedalboard. Practice this and you will begin to feel that there is a balance point involved with both the position of the foot on the pedalboard as well as the balance of weight that keeps the beater off the drum head when you are not playing it.

At this point, the right foot should be nicely balanced with the beater away from the drum head. Each time you strike the head make sure you return to the balance point where the beater is away from the drum head and never leave the beater pressed into the drum head.

Repeat this process a few times to make sure that you have the hang of it. It will take practice at first but the positioning will become second nature after a while. You just need to keep reading the instructions above and then practicing the technique. This is much like the Alexander Technique, as you keep returning to your drum set any positioning your feet and keep thinking about the actions you need to make you will soon become quite confident in playing the pedals.

The exact same process should be repeated with the hi-hat pedal. However, this time the foot needs to sometimes press the pedal down so that the hi-hat cymbals are against each other tightly. Again, there is a balance point where you hold the cymbals together tightly and where you hold them together loosely. A little experience practicing this will soon give you the idea but don't lean forward with your body in order to press the cymbals together tightly as the weight of your leg plus a little pressure should do the trick. Try not to press too tightly with your left foot. Close the cymbals and try pressing a little until the desired sound is heard when you hit the hi-hat cymbals with the tip of the drumstick.

BALANCE!

I have mentioned balance points before now and it serves well to bring it up again at this point - now that you have learned the hands and feet positions, as well as posture concepts.

Again, I cannot stress enough the value of great posture. Back straight, neck aligned, chin up, chest out, shoulders tucked in/down. You then play the drums with hands and feet, not with your neck and back? They are the core and thus should be centralized? Don't worry about getting it wrong at first, just be mindful of how I am describing the posture position and over time you will automatically sit in the correct position.

The importance of the stool also comes into play here. It must be solid and sturdy, comfortable, and set to the right height so that your feet when in the balanced position on the pedalboards lifts your thighs horizontal to the floor.

Now having described the posture and feet positions, hand positions, and balance points of the stick (see accompanying videos) it will further help to think about the balance point of the whole of the drummer before hitting anything.

Floating Around the Kit

From this start position as described previously turn to the left (slightly) and see your drums and cymbals placed there and then turn again, this time to the right. Is everything within striking distance of your hands when elbows are positioned relatively close to your sides? If not reposition everything so that all of your drums and cymbals and any additional percussion add-ons are as tight and close as possible and therefore within easy reach and requires very little effort to hit. But there is a balance here also, don't bring them too close that they become uncomfortable and you become cramped up as you sit and play.

Next, without trying to play the drums get the feel of this central position. Your lower back and buttocks are a kind of pivot or fulcrum point where everything comes from.

Your core.

Move your hands and wrists up and down and around the kit as if playing the drums but don't strike the drums just yet. Do the same thing at the same time with the pedals. Lift your feet off slightly and strike the drum but not deliberately, accidentally. It doesn't matter if you hit the BD or HH slightly but try not to make a sound or very little sound. Don't try to play anything in particular, just hover around the kit.

As you "pretend" to play the drums and just kind of mime your way around the kit (it doesn't matter if you actually hit a drum or cymbal or two) notice this central core position. The pivotal point at your core that takes everything you think to play and transfers it to the kit. This should be a loose position. If not, loosen everything up.

You are in effect hovering over the kit so make your limbs loose and also loosen the grip you may have on your drumsticks. The kit is as one with you and every drum is there, easy to strike and every cymbal is in easy striking position from the drummers' point of view and not, so the kit looks good from the audience's point of view or so they can see your face. You're a drummer, not a model. Unless that's your thing, I won't judge.

Now as you pretend to float loosely around the kit with your hands and feet, begin to play something. A basic rock style beat for instance. It doesn't matter if you can't play anything yet, just get used to hitting the drums without too much energy.

However, keep the floating going. Don't hit the drums as hard as you can. Simply float your way around the beat and the position while you're playing. Then try a simple fill. Keep the floating flowing motion going. It sounds crazy but this exercise is mostly about not playing the drums as you in-fact play them.

When you add dynamic accents to your playing and power hits at various points in your playing while still keeping the balance at your core and the floating motion going your playing will begin to sound smooth and yes, floating or smooth, controlled, and in time. Play the time from this vantage point and you will begin to sound great even playing basic rhythms and beats fills and solos.

This is akin to Bruce Lee's art of fighting without fighting. You are fluidlike so become the kit. This is also about not putting too much energy into the exercise. Practice these motions every month or so as your drumming develops. The reason being that this is the mind part of drumming. It is the place you should aim for after you have had your head down in the kit for a while practicing the exercises and lessons within the Time Space & Drums Series, but by the time you complete the first Rock Foundation book you will be able to return to the floating concept and play something but because you have practiced you can begin to play more loosely and as suggested floating. It will take practice but you will begin to see the benefits as you develop your skills.

Mind Over Body!

I've already talked about the balanced floating technique. However, I think it's important to note one important detail. This floating or balance is really a balance between mind and body, the art and the science.

To illustrate, if I were to give a non-drummer a pair of sticks and then asked him to play the drums, he would be automatically acting from a mental point of view, or unconsciously.

He has never played the drums so has no reference point so he automatically floats around the kit and makes a noise. In an attempt to impress he will refer or invoke from memory some drumming he has heard at some time in the past and try to interpret or mimic what he recalls. This will sometimes come across as rigid, jerky, loud and noisy, or just plain wrong. As he does this, he will automatically move from mind to body in an attempt to improve what he is playing and make it sound better.

Again, what the non-drummer has unknowingly done is make a journey from mind to body or art to the science in an attempt to play something cool as he invokes associations from memory, and of course, because he hasn't practiced anything he comes up with very little.

Now I mention this because superb drummers play 95% of their drumming unconsciously and automatically, creatively and artistically but of course the playing is guided by their conscious minds. This being an effect of their years of practicing and training or what I refer to here as the science of drumming.

Think of it like this, if you got in your car to drive 50 miles down the road you would in most cases be driving automatically because you learned to drive 10 or more years ago so driving is automatic for you.

Very rarely do you have to think about what you are actually doing?

From this, it is clear to see that in order to become a great drummer we need to practice the theoretical science of it, and that job doesn't get done watching endless videos. Through analysis of your own playing and constant constructive criticism, you learn your instrument and later become great or an automatic (great) player.

That isn't to say that you lack control at that point because constant practice and improvement make sure that you have complete control through the scientific or conscious thought that goes into your practice and playing times.

So, mind over body or mind over matter can only take place after the body has learned the science (the body of drumming). Then the mind over body part comes into play as you play great things automatically or from your unconscious memory. In that, we see that the mental part of the equation is an automatic effect of mastering the body or science part, much like the artistic side of the drummer is an effect of mastering the science. Both concepts are integrally interchangeable.

After developing the science to the highest degree possible you have in effect programmed yourself to be a great drummer.

It is a vital journey all beginners and masters should traverse, conscious - practice - practice - practice. Ring any bells? It should, but it must be a self-disciplined conscious effort and practice and not undisciplined unconscious wandering around the thing we are practicing. Your unconscious is like another you trying to push you off target so you need to discipline it as you would a young child in order to bring it into obedience or control through conscious effort towards a predetermined result or goal.

The Science and Art of Drumming!

It seems from our very beginnings we are taught about dualities and opposites. God and Satan, right and wrong, good and bad, man and woman, positive and negative, up and down, right and left, back and front and on and on and on it goes.

What we don't readily see within each of the opposites mentioned and the ones not mentioned is that there is always a vantage point from where the subject is viewed. i.e. right is only right viewed from the left. Viewed from the right that same place becomes left.

Think about this and you'll discover that there really are no opposites at all. However, it is essential for the opposites to exist in order to make an informed judgment about the subject matter. A reference point that helps keep us safe from harm has to be created.

For instance, if one didn't know cold from hot water one could put oneself in danger, place your hand in the hot water and most likely burn yourself. But paradoxically if you put your hand in freezing water that may also burn. Of course, it's a different kind of burning sensation but you get the picture. Knowledge of opposites is essential as one integrally links with the other but the theory must be known and understood and then known and understood from a different perspective if the theory requires it.

As drummers, we need to concern ourselves with the **Science** of Drums and the **Art** of Drums. Two distinct opposites. As well as the **Theory** of Music and the **Practice** of Music, again, two opposites.

We need to fully examine and assimilate the theory in order to make better use of the practice. That practice must, in the beginning, be scientifically applied and practiced in order to master the theory and practice of drumming - in order to be seen from the outside world as creative, artistic, and eventually master of the art of drumming.

If you don't know what to practice you need a guide. A teacher will teach you the requirements but a guide will show you the way as previously mentioned. That isn't necessarily true of a teacher but as in all things they are very much linked together.

Like most authorities in life, the teacher can hide information and manipulate the student along his path in order to profit from the student. The authority belongs to the teacher but in reality, the authority should always be with the student. This requires a guide and not a teacher and again we see that it is the perspective you take that often determines the difference.

A guide reveals the path - which is what is required by the student in order for him to become his own authority and master, as well as the teacher.

He himself needs to develop the ear in order to know that what he plays is either performed well or badly. Only then can he become the master and teacher through constant analysis and mastery over each segment of knowledge he studies, himself, and his participation and use of the knowledge he puts into practice.

And as mentioned previously he must do this scientifically in a conscious fashion.

Only with the self-discipline to practice what is needed does he prevail.

He may then receive comments from the outside world such as, "What an artist"? but remember, that the art is an effect of a well-executed science! A science that the subject as been mastering over a long period.

From the Beginning to The End and Back!

If you read carefully the Creating A Universe - In the Beginning document received free with the Rock Drumming Foundation book you will discover that it outlines the description of the creation of the universe.

That creation process contains a beginning, an explosive, or expansive period, followed by an implosion period and eventually an end.

The major growth stage is the explosion and the major development/improvement period is the implosion. All in All:

- The Beginning – The primal cause (or goal).

- The Explosion – Causes (plural? meaning the goals put into action).

- The Implosion - Working on the effect of the causes and bringing them all together.

- The End - The final effect or result.

The final effect is continually integrating with another beginning followed by another ending and so on. It's a never-ending cycle of creation and from the drummers' point of view continued improvement. That cycle can either be a negative cycle (lack of practice and planning) or a positive cycle. Planned Practice, Preparation, and Development.

In the world of improvement, you are always at the beginning which is why the master teachers of drumming and anything else are students themselves? In fact, they are the very best students?

This same cycle is present in all growth. Think about nature for a minute, you plant the seed, you grow the fruit, you harvest the fruit and you receive the fruit or reward which contains within it the seed of the fruits of the future. Or next year's harvest.

All ideas start out as an idea then the idea is developed, Improvements are made and profits received, financial or otherwise. I refer to profits here as results or effects - good or bad? Examine the processes in your life and you will discover this same cycle in just about all the things that you do.

A seed is planted, a baby is born, the baby grows to maturity and passes away but before the person passed away, he left his seed for further growth and so on.

THE BEGINNING

Knowing this cycle exists, it makes sense after the initial idea to become a great drummer or anything else is conceived that a detailed plan and list of what's needed should be created as part of that beginning in order to develop the idea to its best and fullest potential.

The technique can then be developed later to improve the standard of your drumming to finally reap the rewards earned throughout the cycle or cycles, current or new cycles. In the beginning, at least, the technique should be viewed much like the water you give to your plants. You feed them in the beginning, in our case learn some basic techniques, and intermittently throughout the growth cycle where you constantly practice and improve, you feed on the water as you go, meaning that you add a little technique to your practice that will get you to the next step.

Section 3

The Kit

Your First Kit

Basic Needs and Requirement!

Moving away from the drummer and onto the drums themselves, it helps when choosing a drum kit to know what you're going to be doing on it - what you are going to be practicing, your goals and aims. However, luckily there is a universal setup which can also be built into a larger kit at a later date should you so wish.

We will use the junior kit image above as our starting point and example. I will list the items the kit contains and their basic use and whether or not they can be removed from the kit to create a smaller set.

Usually the answer to the question, can we remove this part of the drum kit? in this case will be no and for very good reason from a practical point of view.

Basic Necessities

A good understanding of the following drums and drum parts is essential and so I will include a brief reason why.

1 - The Stool or Drum Throne. The kit above contains a drum throne or drum stool. Of course, we need that item and we cannot remove it unless the drummer plays from an armchair which is not very practical. The point of a good drum stool is that they are height adjustable so we can set the height to suit us personally.

Some kits don't come with a stool so always make sure that there is one included in the kit you eventually plan to buy. You will hopefully be spending a lot of time at your new drum kit so make sure your stool is good quality and it is a comfortable one.

2 - Snare Drum. The snare drum is the heart of any drum kit. It is the central point where everything else grows from. Marching drummers just use a snare drum which enables them to become very good rudimentary players if they are serious in their drumming but they do have the perfect opportunity to practice rudiments. They master the basic rudiments because just like the snare drum is the heart of a drum kit, rudiments are the heart of the marching drummer's arsenal.

So, it makes sense that the three hearts meet and become properly acquainted, yours and your snare drums, as well as your rudiments.

The message here is master the rudiments in the one area of the snare drum, to begin with, but remember this is an integrated skill which integrates with foot technique too if you plan to develop as far as possible.

I mention rudiments here and the fact that you should master them but remember rudiments are a lifelong pursuit and will take time to completely master.

3 - Bass Drum. This part of the kit is another essential ingredient as it forms the foundation of most rhythms and conveys a pulse along with the other drum parts like the left foot hi-hat. The bass drum is the "bottom end" so to speak, but almost always used to promote or convey the pulse where a pulse is required.

4 - Hi-Hat - The left foot hi-hat cymbals are the primary pulse creator for most rhythms and again is an invaluable part of the drum kit. Played with the left foot it conveys the pulse of the beat and can be played either open with the foot lifted slightly or closed with the foot pressed down on the pedal to different and varying pressures or degrees depending on the music you are playing at the time as this gives the ability to play tightly or loosely as well as quietly or with a much louder rock type feel.

5 – Tom-Toms - Usually a basic kit includes 3 tom-toms in total - 2 Mounted on the bass drum and one floor-tom-tom. The floor tom-tom stands on 3 legs on the floor to the right of a right-handed player as he/she sits behind the kit but over recent years these tom-toms are usually mounted on a clamp either to a dedicated stand or drum rack for instance. Some jazz drummers do remove the mid-tom from the bass drum and that is fine except the exercises within the Time Space and Drums series are written as if there are three tom-toms in the kit, however, if you just have one tom you can quite easily adapt.

Tom-toms are fillers that are usually used to play fills between each endpoint leading into various parts or sections of a song such as verse, chorus, middle sections, etc. Of course, you can always play rhythms on the tom-toms too, Indian type rhythms for example. But remember that this is the most basic use and description only aimed at the complete beginner.

6 - Ride Cymbal and Crash Cymbals - The kit above contains one essential combination crash/ride cymbal. It can be used to play both crashes into new song sections as well as phrasing throughout the music piece. Also, the ride cymbal is usually used in combination with the open and closed hi-hat to keep the time in basic rhythms and beyond. Most drummers, however, do usually prefer to have a dedicated ride cymbal as they generally sound much better.

Hi-Hat PULSE – As mentioned above the hi-hat as well as being played with the left foot pressed against the foot pedal is usually the main engine that drives the pulse and keeps time for the rest of the band and the drummer usually by playing the quarter notes or pulse with the left foot.

The above-mentioned drum parts are the essential minimum ingredients of a great drum kit. However, it should be born in mind that although the above-mentioned parts each have a basic use, they can also be played in lots of different ways limited only by your personal imagination and creativity.

Different nuances around the kit are used to project the drummer's dynamics and technique to the listener which in most part promotes and supports the pulse of the particular song being played.

Apart from sticks and the willpower to practice, the above list contains all of the basic ingredients of any good drum kit. Of course, other drums and cymbals can be added at a later date should you require them.

Quality Sound!

Each of the five drums included in a basic kit setup should have a great drum head or drum skin to create the best quality sound and get the best out of the drum itself. Usually, drum kits come with good quality heads from the offset. It is, however, a requirement that each of the heads is replaced as and when they need replacing - usually after a few months hard bashing.

It must be said that tuning a drum the right way and then striking it the right way makes for the best quality sound and assists the life of a drum head.

DRUM TUNING!

In order for you to get a head start and before you begin more in-depth studies and practices involved in learning to play the drums, you need to solve the problem of tuning and how to get a great sound out of any drum.

From this point, it should, therefore, be enough to simply check and refine each drum to make sure that it produces the sound you like. If they require retuning and cannot be brought into obedience by making a few basic quick changes schedule this so as to not default from your normal practice and development time.

How the kit sounds, is really a personal preference but as I mentioned earlier, I believe every drum, although can be tuned to get almost any kind of sound out of it, has its own preferred sound based on the drum material and its individual uniqueness and characteristics. You will get a feel for what I mean after some practice and experience tuning the drums for yourself. We will discuss this later.

FELT BEATERS

I personally never use a bass drum beater that has the hard plastic to the head of the drum. It seems too harsh a sound for me when used to hit the bass drum. It is also more likely to damage the drum head.

Again, this is a personal decision of mine, yours may differ so go with what sounds and feels good to you.

I prefer the felt beaters. Not the really soft stuff but the hard felt as this provides a solid and rich deep sound without the click of the harder plastic material and the fluffiness of softer wool type materials. Hard felt is my choice here. Wooden beaters are also out for me personally, but I suppose it depends on the type of music you prefer to play. Really heavy music may require harder beaters if you prefer them but I very rarely play heavy rock anymore.

NYLON TIPS

To me plastic or nylon tipped drumsticks don't belong in drumming for the same reasons as fluffy felt beaters or harsher materials for the bass drum pedal beater. They seem to harsh when hitting the drum or cymbal with the stick but as I suggested for the beater type it would completely depend on the music you are playing at the time.

My preferred stick is something like the "Vic Firth 5A" sized stick. It's not too light and not too heavy and provides me with ease of use and more control. Heavier sticks are just that, heavy, and I want things easy.

Again, as before try a few sticks on your drums and cymbals to find your own preference and don't be afraid to copy what someone else does if that suits you better, or until you find a better choice yourself.

Strike Up the Beat - OR NOT?

The technique of striking the drum the right way has been explained in so many different ways and each attempt to describe the technique boils down to one rather silly phrase. To not hit the drum when you're hitting it? Yes, I know - I feel like a fool even as I write it.

In short, you go for it when striking the drum then let it go and let the stick bounce onto (not into) and then off of the drum head on its own. In short, it is a loose grip and so controlling the bounce of the stick as it leaves the drum head, then preparing to strike it again with another bounce is the real technique.

The Point

I mention the above for one reason which is that the drum makes the sound. The drummer does not. The drum has a certain sound at which it resonates perfectly. This is more evident in more expensive drum sets but true of all drums in general.

Usually, after a long time learning to tune the drums although you could get it straight away, you can usually make any drum sound great or more aptly put - get the best out of any drum.

In this respect, it goes without saying that all drums manufactured today in most part are great drums. Getting the best sound possible out of the drum is the real art of the drummer through both his playing and tuning techniques.

As in life, the saying Success Breeds Success is apt here as quality playing (hitting the drum the right way) begets quality sounds? That phrase is true whether or not the environment the kit is in is conducive to playing the drums.

For example, even the most expensive drum kit would require some gaffer tape intervention in a large hall creating lots of ring from the drum in question unless of course, that is the sound you like to hear and of course until people packed the place out then the sound would change somewhat.

A pillow in the bass drum slightly touching the beater side and possibly a little tape on the heads and so on, usually leads to a great sound. This all requires experimentation on your part so try different things for yourself in a variety of environments if possible, to find what you like and what works for you.

This is not a technique book so the above information regarding hitting the drum should be added to any other technique you read about or watch on various videos. That said, there is only one video I have ever watched that goes into tuning a drum the right way and as well as teaching the basic rudiments and holding the sticks, etc. and that is Dave Weckl's Back to Basics video. I highly recommend that video to run alongside any other learning aid you make use of especially the Time Space and Drums Series.

Please also note that any resources I recommend from time to time are from various sources for which Time Space & Drums do receive a very small commission... or my own sites directly related to the Time Space and Drums series, blog posts to aid your studies for instance. But remember that I only recommend the legitimate top of the range quality materials for study purposes. I do not recommend anything simply to make money as for me this is about providing as much value as I can to you the reader/student/teacher whichever the case may be.

That said, there's nothing wrong with making money, in fact, if you want to make a full-time career out of your drumming then, by all means, make money where and when you can. It can only aid you in attaining more books and programs that help you become even better.

Looking ahead to Your Uniqueness!

As a growing drummer your own unique style will develop and thus your drum kit will develop with you should you desire – but it's important to note that the basic 5-piece kit is recommended to support your growth at the start. If your budget is low or non-existent, I have mentioned in other parts of this book about starting with no kit at all. Just keep reading to find out how and then develop your skills as you save in order to attain the best kit possible for your current or future budget and situation.

The basic 5-piece drum kit allows for all of the basic functionality, practice, and learning as well as provides plenty of room to grow in your own musical direction for either more fun or to support your developing unique drumming style.

Don't Forget the Fun!

As with most directions in life, musical or other - you are bound to make mistakes and wrong decisions - It's a part of the human experience to search and find the target answers and solutions in any given direction and with any particular goal we aim to reach. Those so-called mistakes are then, not really mistakes at all, and in drumming the mistakes you make usually lead to the more creative side of your unique style emerging.

So, although perfection is or can be part of the learning and mastery process - perfection as nothing to do with starting out on the drums. Mistakes will be made and plenty of fun will be had whilst making those mistakes and I am sure there will be plenty of frustrations solving them but, in the end, they will all eventually lead to a brilliantly unique drumming style all of your own.

This is now going slightly off-topic and more into the self-development arena which of course has its place in any area including drumming. But for now, let's get back on topic and I'll mention a few more things that will help develop your particular style.

If you're a junior drummer just starting out, the fun will most likely be the order of the day - which is fine, and if just having fun is your aim then more fun to you.

Sound Quality

If you remember, earlier I mentioned the subject of "Sound Quality" which again forms part of your unique style. Tuning the drums high, low, ringing or dead, deep and loud or high and short all make for your own unique style which when recognized should be developed further through learning and developing in directions that support your unique style.

This is part of the growth and development process and should be born in mind from the start. If you like something whether it's a sound or a kit setup go for it and see where it leads you.

The way in which the drum is struck again plays a part in creating a style all of your own. Maybe you're a hard hitter or a gentle giant. That is, until the moment you hear a sound you play that strikes you and then helps your playing ability go up a little until eventually your whole drumming ability is raised to greater heights to support that one thing you did that struck a note in your heart and added something special to your particular playing style. Check out Terry Bozzio for something completely out of the ordinary yet completely brilliant.

Either way, whether you have a creative insight or a purely scientific approach to hitting and tuning the drums that assist your uniqueness surface - you will end up as unique as you really and truly are. But also remember that being creative is really about being scientific at first. By that I mean you must first learn the science of something before the creative side can emerge. How else would you play something that is beyond you at present? as a drummer and person. You will then realize that the drum kit is a part of your personality which is jumping the gun a little but still quite true.

In short, it is later as we develop that we see clearly that the errors we made, in the beginning, were the defining moments that lead to an enhanced playing style, more success, and a very unique way of playing the drums. And by errors, I simply mean small things you did that made a big difference in your playing style and therefore your sound.

Built to Last & Room for Development

It's important in drumming to have the very best quality drums and hardware you can afford. This is especially true when buying a Junior Drum Kit for yourself or your child.

It is important that the drum kit you buy supports yours or your child's growth in both size and quality standards. Then, as your child outgrows the drum kit it would possibly be sold or locked away in the garage or worse.

However, if the drums were of such a high standard as to serve as additions to a full-sized drum kit a few years later then the drums may not be a total right-off.

We believe the general lower budget 5-piece drum kits available today are of such a good standard that they will usually last for many years to come whether you decide to upgrade in the future or not, at least as a first starter drum kit. In general, most full size and junior drum kits available today are built very well and in most cases:

1 - They have all the basic requirements. Snare drum, bass drum, three tom-toms, crash/ride cymbal, and hi-hat cymbal - All of the hardware and stool are usually included which makes for an ideal and complete package and therefore the ideal choice for junior drummers who are just starting out and want the very best value for money possible.

2 - They're built to high manufacturing specifications. In today's product production line (get em out there as fast as possible) environment it's easy to lower standards due to high demand. But in most cases, modern drum kits are built to good standards throughout and have quality drums and hardware all-around.

3 - Ideal entry-level kit - Room for development - While being Junior drum kits and due mainly to the high manufacturing level of precision these standard kits have the potential for growth. For example, if it is your child that has the drumming bug so to speak, and you realize at some point that the drum kit is becoming too small and their growth literally outgrows the junior drum set - It can be used as additions to a newer more suitable drum kit. This is an option simply because of the high standard of the lower end junior drum kits available today.

Of course, there are many great junior drum kits if you're buying for a child or young relative so keep within your budget and understand that your first kit is at best a stepping stone to something much better as you become more confident about yourself or your child's commitment and development into the future.

Then you can look at higher-priced drum kits such as Pearl, Tama, Ludwig, DW, and Yamaha to name a few. These are superb drum kits each having various standards and types from low-range to mid-range right up to high-end kits. You can also be sure that these kits will last a lifetime if you look after them.

Long Practice? Silent Practice

Whatever drum kit you choose, practicing the drums can be a bit of noise for the drummer, the family members, and the neighborhood. Of course, this won't be such an issue if you live in a detached house in the country and have your drum kit set up in the garage across the yard but unfortunately, that isn't usually the case.

So, there are a few things to consider before buying a drum kit, junior or full size. A few ideas, options and considerations follow to help you prepare for buying the drum kit of your choice.

Lower the Decibels

Decibels are the unit of noise volume measurement and without looking on the internet I think anything over 80db is considered anti-social and therefore, needs attention.

The heading to this section of this book is Long Practice with a "?" A question mark is used because Long Practice requires some thought on your part. And in order to do any amount of Long Practice the list below will help keep the neighbors at bay, your family happy and your ears protected from noise damage.

1 - Ear Protection. The first consideration is ear protection. A good set of earplugs is essential to the drummer serious about playing the drums simply because long term practice can damage the eardrums so earplugs should be used during every practice session. Earplugs have an added advantage for the drummer which only becomes apparent when studying and practicing more seriously. That is, when wearing earphones or earplugs, it helps block the minds focus on the outside world and helps the drummer to focus on what he is practicing. For me at least, this little psychological trick helped me to focus more inwardly and on the sound that was being produced and my part in producing that sound.

2 - Sound Proofing. The drum kit and especially the drum practice environment should be adequately soundproofed if at all possible when practicing the drums for long periods. The reasons are obvious but with the addition of helping the drum kit to sound good. Egg cartons or carpets on the wall, for instance, are particularly good and an alternative to egg cartons is used in real studio environments. But bear in mind that sound vibrates so people in your local vicinity may still get annoyed at the vibrations caused by long practice sessions.

3 - Practice Pads. Practicing the drums can be more gratifying without any dampening such as with rubber practice pads. However, when it comes to long serious practice, having practice pads can be helpful in a few ways. They make the drum stroke instant with no ring. This helps the drummer to perfect the timing of his drum stokes to perfection. Drumming then becomes a more theoretical scientific endeavor rather than an artistic one.

4 - Practice Kits - A real practice kit or electronic kit can be slightly more practical in size and can be a lot quieter than standard drum practice pads (the type of practice pads that are placed on each drum). They also have more bounce due to manufacturers endeavoring to create a real drum kit feel. This makes electronic kits ideal for serious long hours of study and practice along the path to drumming success.

An important thing to note here is that there is a difference in practice and playing music. Playing music is an effect of the scientific study and practice of drumming for which a practice kit really is best at least some of the time. Playing music is the art, or application of the practice, practicing drums is the science...

5 - Rudimentary Practice Time - If it becomes too much of an issue to practice the drums at home the alternative is to purchase a dedicated practice pad (the single snare drum type). These rubber pads are ideal for in-depth snare drum rudimentary practice.

Rudiments form the whole basis of drumming so when the rudiments are great - the drumming isn't far behind. Along with drum kit coordination and independence practice, all drummers should make regular use of a practice pad to develop the basic rudiments to the highest standard possible.

6 - Dampening - A little gaffer tape on the edge of each drum head can be great to eliminate unwanted ringtones from the drum. Experiment with different size strips of gaffer tape to find the perfect sound for you. A small pillow or piece of foam in the bottom of a bass drum can further muffle the noise of a kit and make for better deeper sounds from the bass drum. Experiment again with different sized cushions or pillows, usually the softer the pillow the better which is why I don't use the foam option. The bass drum only needs slight dampening not killing the sound all together but that goes for all the drums. The idea is to make the drum sound good and not to kill the sound altogether.

7 - Pillows/Cushions - Finding a suitable cushion to practice snare drum rudiments on can be great for wrist and arm development. There is very little bounce from the cushion so the drummer has to do all of the work and perfect his/her drum stroke. In this case, harder cushions are best but experiment again to find a perfect surface to enable you to prolong your practice time. We will touch on this subject further later in this book.

Some or all of the techniques above can greatly help the drummer control his environment rather than being controlled by it and its demands.

I hope you have found something of use in this section and that you employ some or all of its advice enabling you to Practice for Longer Periods. However, always take regular breaks after 30 minutes or so.

This helps freshen the mind and helps focus on better results. An accelerated learning technique is to take regular breaks because the mind more easily simulates what you did at the end of a session. Therefore, add regular endings to your sessions by taking lots of 5, 10, 15, or 30-minute breaks. You then approach the next practice session with a much clearer focus.

Playing for Fun - Playing Vs Practice

All of the ideas and concepts discussed so far will hopefully help the beginner get more out of their drumming including having more fun whilst playing the drums.

Creating the right environment and getting the best sound out of each drum helps the drum to sound its very best and so, as the drummer your job is to find the drums perfect sound. The better the sound the more enjoyment you will get from playing that drum or sound. Try to spend a little time getting the drums to sound good and the more fun you will have when it comes to playing them.

Even the most expensive drums on the market need care in setting up in order to get the best out of them.

Practice Versus Playing

I understand that having fun on the drum kit can be easily attainable by pretending to be Buddy Rich or some other great drummer. That can be lots of fun but what's much more fun is actually sounding like those great drummers.

What I mean is: Practice and Playing are two different things. Long practice in the manner already discussed makes for a better drummer and therefore better playing.

Learning at least the very basics is definitely the road to take whether you want to have some fun or you are more serious about becoming better on the drums.

Practice is the time you dedicate to getting better or developing your drumming skill. This can be done on a rudiment practice pad, a practice kit, or on the acoustic or electronic drum kit. This part of drumming is disciplined by you and controlled by you. It is time spent reaching for a particular goal or aim that you have previously set for yourself.

Playing is the time you spend either performing for a crowd or yourself. Playing is the integration of all of your practiced skills into a coherent whole.

As an individual, you may have more fun and get more enjoyment out of practicing than playing. Your own likes and dislikes and personality will give you clues as to what you enjoy and what you don't. But I hope that you become serious and would like to develop your drumming skills for years to come and become the very best you can possibly be.

Whatever level you are currently at set yourself some basic goals, to begin with so you can progressively move towards specific goals within your drumming practice time. The effect is that you get more fun out of your playing.

The Time Space & Drums series integrates with what needs to be done and when it needs doing as you develop your drumming skills and so whether you're a complete beginner or intermediate player the goal of completing the series is set out in bite-sized steps from the book you now hold in your hands moving onto the Rock Drumming Foundation book and beyond. The outcome of that completed goal would be that you are now a great drummer.

Roadmap to Success!

It may seem a little or a lot premature to begin thinking about long term goals, aims, or plans to drumming success but really, we are still talking about the first step down the road to success and drumming mastery through mastering Time and Space. What we do and where we do it so to speak and so it makes sense to set up some goals from the start that give us a better and clearer road ahead.

The First Step in The Right Direction

Once all of the beginning goals are set and the start-up problems are solved regarding noise control, budgets, and other issues of practicing - of course, the first step to success is **choosing the right drum kit**, and **the right tuition or learning process**. Those two choices will set you toward the goal you aspire to.

All of the other additional concepts and strategies we have discussed throughout this book are optional. The more they are implemented into the two mentioned steps of:

    1 - Choosing the Right Drum Kit.

    2 - Choosing the Right Learning Method.

The more success and fun the complete beginner, as well as the intermediate drummer, will have.

But there is just one other thing to consider. That would be mixing with other like-minded people and drummers who are all on the same road to drumming success and with similar but varied aims and goals within the exciting world of drumming.

To that end, I am in the process of creating and developing the Time Space and Drums Community so you can speak to other drummers just starting out - ask others for advice or give your advice to other members. The community is hosted at timespaceanddrums.me but the site title is really Time Space Drums and You.

Interacting with like-minded people and sharing ideas is a fantastic additional feature available to the beginning drummer today and one that every drummer should take advantage of.

You can join a growing community of drummers willing to share their know-how and tips with other community members. As a member of this growing community, you could become a drum guru yourself and give others valuable advice.

Section 4

Evolving Beyond the Basics

Beginner Tips

In this next section of this beginner drumming concepts and tips book, we're going to cover how to solve some of the many problems associated with learning how to play the drums. The problems have become associated with drums for obvious reasons but the solutions to those problems are just as obvious and far more rewarding to your end result and progress along your drumming journey once you integrate them into your practices.

With a little effort on your part, these solutions will get you out there practicing and improving your drumming knowledge and skill level mostly without problems occurring.

FRESH AIR, the Greatest Value to Human Life & Drummers.

I was recently made aware of the fact that a lot of drummers without the facilities and equipment to begin learning to play the drums would quite literally play the air around them and would literally practice to thin air. This isn't such a crazy idea as it might at first sound. It brings into focus a very important part of becoming a great drummer. Understanding.

Understanding - although mentioned here as a virtue and a supreme one at that, is also the cause of a very great problem, and I don't want to dis anyone here but the lack of understanding of the fundamental knowledge regarding drumming is the cause of many drummers having a great affinity to *"learning how to play the drums"* from videos.

Don't get me wrong, videos have their place and are a vital way of learning at the beginning. But, after a few short drumming demonstrations on video giving you the ability to see where the hand positions are as well as the feet when playing certain basic fundamentals, videos themselves become a problem. If you doubt my sincerity in that look at the greatest drummer who ever lived and the technology around at those times.

Of course, I am speaking of Buddy Rich and the likes of Jene Krupa and Louis Belson. Those great drummers didn't have access to videos and DVDs, for the most part at least, and I am almost sure the great drummers of today don't sit around watching drumming videos. Dave Weckl and Chad Wackerman just to name two.

Those players are busy getting better in themselves and their lives. I am just guessing here but next time you watch a YouTube video ask yourself if Buddy Rich would do this. Indeed, his famous quote was that the only way to get better at playing drums is to play the drums. Not watch someone else do it.

There is one exception to that rule which we will touch upon later, now back to point.

The videos become a problem because drumming is about music and music is heard. Music is not seen? That said, it should become even more apparent that it is of vital importance to develop the ear of the drummer and to do that requires a basic theoretical understanding of drumming, music, and theory. Yes, videos include music too but the listener takes on a more passive role as he tries to absorb new knowledge and material.

These are my own personal opinions and I am sure many drummers would argue the facts but most likely they have a vested interest in you watching their videos. Again, don't get me wrong, videos are awesome and great learning tools but after the initial learning stages are over you would be better served sitting at a drum kit and working things out between yourself, your kit and the book are learning from at the time whether or not it is one of my own or another more advanced book. In most cases, drummers teach a certain method for a good reason usually pertaining to what they themselves have learned, practiced, and more importantly experienced, and come to mention it don't ever let anyone tell you that knowledge is power. Experience beats knowledge hands down, so learn from the experienced drummers if you can seek them out. My apologies for the rant but you needed to know. Now, where was I? ah yes...

So, after studying and getting to a state of understanding of the basic theory of music, in particular, drum music exercises and drum charts, we as drummers begin to take that understanding and begin a process often overlooked by many drummers who could quite easily become great.

That process is taking the theory, or knowledge and integrating it with our minds to further increase our drumming theory neural pathways and therefore understanding.

This may all sound very advanced and very complicated but it really isn't as you will soon discover. We study and learn to a state of understanding then we bring that understanding into clear focus in a visualized form. I could quite easily have stated that it is the visualization that is the supreme value but it is the visualizing that gives better understanding not the other way around.

The images we create in our minds of the drumming theories and concepts, what they mean, and what we associate with them *(This Is the practical application, of the visualized exercise or concept)* determines the result we achieve in both understandings followed by our practical application of that understanding.

THE BIG PICTURE

This is why reading over watching is so vital in any learning process. We begin to form images in our minds as we read of the theories and concepts we are reading about.

Now that we see the big picture of this chunk of information regarding drumming and drumming improvement, we begin to see the simple cycle of:

Learn it -> **Study it** *(memorize it)* -> come to **Understand it** -> **Visualise it** - **Play it**—automatically at will. Notice the paradox here between what I said earlier about visualizing coming first and not the understanding.

Once we begin that process and we begin to see the effect it has on our playing we become better drummers with the more fundamental knowledge and understanding at times than our ability to practically apply it.

Again, don't get dismayed as you will discover everything that I write here works integrally with each other concept. The theory, the visualizing, the practice, the listening, and the rudiments, etc. Everything is about integration and not division as we are often taught in drumming. "Split it up and you can learn it piece by piece," they say. That isn't true because if we cannot play it, that means that it is already split up. See my post on Integration and Division For more info. (http://bit.ly/2UTAwoN).

The simple truth is that the human body works better when the mind is in sync with it and that comes into the picture through visualizing what we are doing and what we are going to do.

As a practical illustration, if you have watched F1 racing and a safety car is brought out, as the safety car is going to go back into the pits and the race is about to begin afresh - the engineer will sometimes say to the driver "Sebastian (?) think about the fresh start and visualize what you are going to do". This is preparation for success! Or more aptly - Controlling the outcome, and all athletes do this. It is essentially claiming success at the beginning of the journey ahead and not being a slave to that same journey and the possible random outcomes.

In short - picture yourself doing it perfectly through understanding the theory - this is essentially getting intellectual understanding along with imaginative control. If you cannot create a picture in your mind of an exercise or concept you probably cannot play the exercise, or at the least play it well. That is because consciousness works through creating concepts which in most cases are nuggets of truths that we perceive in image form in our minds.

 **TASK:** The task here is simply to learn some theory and then become intimately acquainted with that theory. Whenever you learn a new concept simply think and reflect on it until you can form clear images in your mind of the theory or concept. This is essentially creating memories in image form and recalling those images at will which becomes a powerful tool.

Bringing Inner Understanding into Solid Reality.

JUST STICKS!

You can begin learning drums (and you should begin learning this way in the beginning if you're on a tight budget) by spending as little as $10 on a good set of drumsticks. In the beginning, start with a pair of 5A drum sticks then if you want lighter sticks then you can try a pair of 7A sticks. You may want to go to your local music store to test a few to see which works best for you.

To help guide you in your choice the number refers to the thickness of the stick and so a 5A stick is slightly thicker than a 7A and a 2A stick is much thicker. The letter describes the taper of the butt or shoulder of the stick but really the first number is the thing you should concentrate on to make sure that you are not playing with far too heavy sticks.

You can then use a pillow to practice. Any pillow will do but try to get one of the harder ones that have a little response to your hitting it with the stick. The idea here is to simply begin to develop some basic arm movements and rudiments. Practice each one given in the rudiment's sections at the back of each of the Time Space & Drums series then move onto the next one when you're comfortable.

Although this seems pointless at the beginning it will help you to develop the basic movements of the arms and wrists and become acquainted with the various sticking's used within the rudiments.

Then add different exercises and practice all of the ones that you learn over the period of a month. You should then begin to see some great progress. The point is as always here to practice in a scientifically mathematically exact way to a metronome at a slow speed so you can learn the arms and wrist movements and build strength and skill over time.

This kind of practice is akin to weightlifting and although the, "begin slowly and build up speed process" is included (integrated) here, the added difficulty (less bounce from the sticks) will actually help you to develop your arms and wrist movements. This is about the motions only in order to begin programming your muscle memory so try to be theoretically exact as mentioned earlier in the Hands Position in Section 1 of this book as well as in the Rock Drumming Foundation book.

Make your arms and wrists flow and play the exercises slowly, there is no rush. Playing slowly is actually the best way to learn anything at the beginning.

You can then get yourself a metronome for $10 - $20 once you have practiced the basic movements for a week or two or you can use an online metronome or app.

In this method and following this path you begin to improve as a drummer and solve many of the problems associated with starting to learn to play drums before you even get a kit.

- You begin on a small budget.
- You annoy no-one with the noise.
- You learn the important practical rudiments and stickings.
- You become intimately acquainted with the basic foundational knowledge and theory.

TASK: The task here is simply to learn some sticking exercises. You don't need to perfect them at this point as you will discover that perfecting the rudiments is a lifetime job as there is always room for improvement. Try just practicing each hand individually as you hit the cushion, then use alternate sticking at different speeds but remember this is just until you can get yourself a kit or practice pads.

More Improvement Tips

PRACTICE PADS

OK, so you have some basic sticking's down and you're ready to further improve your hand technique. The next step is to invest in a practice pad.

You should bear in mind that a practice pad will create a little more noise than a cushion but still much less than a real kit or snare drum.

However, you will be able to hear the exercises and rudiments that you play clearly and begin to lock into the metronome. At this point, you should have a metronome you can hear physically outwardly and through headphones. I believe that both types of metronome practice are useful and so practice with and without headphones.

About Speed. Regarding the concept of speed – For now at least, ignore it. The task here is to improve what you have been practicing on the pillows and attain more skill and perfection with those exercises. Increased perfection will only come through slow, disciplined well thought out practice. I recommend 60bpm (beats per minute) as a good starting point and slower if you can manage it but slower tempos are really better left until you are practicing various hand and feet coordination exercises. The aim being to space the beats evenly and, on the metronome, click.

Don't worry if at some point you begin to not actually hear the metronome clicks. That simply means that you are getting it right and in-the-pocket as they say. This is what you should strive for as the click or pulse then gets internalized over time.

When you get to the point that you are comfortable try speeding the tempo of the metronome 10 bpm and practicing at that tempo for a while. Then speed it up in increments of 5-10 bpm until it becomes a struggle or what you play becomes messy. Then stop! and start again slowing back down to 25% less than the tempo where you began to struggle and stick to that temp for a while. It is this slowing down that eventually leads you to be able to play faster by allowing you to push forward with the tempo. You cannot play it well enough at 80 bpm if you don't play it well enough at 70 bpm first?

Do not under any circumstances try to play beyond your current level of speed, but instead, slow the metronome back to 60bpm and then start again if you are disciplined enough to do that as playing slower will help in the long run but also try new tempos too.

IMPORTANT NOTE: When you play slowly at 60bpm for a long period you will begin to increase your skills at that particular exercise to a very high degree and you will begin to master the exercise you are working on. Only then should you speed the metronome in 10bpm increments again and stop when you begin to struggle or the playing begins to drag because you cannot keep up with the metronome.

Do not go beyond your current level just to play faster. Speed will come – slowly at first, but it will come. I realize that I am repeating myself but these are really important points to guide you but having said that use common sense to judge for yourself what is right for you. Remember if you are not already you will become the teacher.

At this point, you will really begin to see and then focus on the space between the notes and thus begin to create a smooth flow in your playing.

The Goal is ACCURACY NOT SPEED.

Try practicing each rudiment in your practice sessions for a month, then 3 months, then spend another 3 months practicing all of the rudiments but spending 50% of your practice time on just one. Then change the main rudiment after 1 week, then again and again until you have spent 1 week on each main rudiment (50% of the practice time).

You can then repeat the whole process and spend another week on the main rudiment, and the next, etc. Repeat the process 4 times and then:

Practice each rudiment in a practice session but practice one (the main rudiment of your choice) 50% of the practice time for a month, then move onto the next rudiment over the following month and so on until you have mastered each rudiment.

And please note here that when I say practice all of the rudiments I am referring to the set or rudiments covered within the Rudimentary section at the back of each of the Time Space & Drums books 1-12 as they are enough for at least the first two to three years of your drumming, then add a rudiment every 3 months and make that added rudiment the main rudiment for 50% of the practice time dedicated to rudiments for at least a month before including it as one of your main rudiments. Then focus back on your main rudiments before adding another 3 months down the line.

You should practice rudiments in a scheduled fashion similar to the above-mentioned process that suits you, (the above is just an example) over your drumming lifetime and remember the objective is accuracy and precision and not speed. I have found that speed is an effect of getting it accurate at slower tempos but you may be different so pay close attention to your development and adjust to suit your own abilities and strengths.

The Feet

So far, your investment in drumming has been very little financially and hopefully quite a bit practically. It is now time to make another investment - and you can go two ways with this.

1. Get yourself a bass drum pedal $20 - $100 and a bass drum pedal practice pad. $50 -$100. (You may even get an all in one solution for $100 or so.

2. Get yourself a full practice kit with bass drum pedal $100 - $200 approximately.

The next thing will be to get hold of a set of hi-hat cymbals and hi-hat stand. These will cost anything from $50 - $200 for a starter setup. It would be preferable to take the second option above as you will always have the practice kit available to avoid annoying anyone, even before you buy yourself an acoustic kit.

ADDING THE BASS DRUM PRACTICE

Once you have the equipment mentioned above it's really time to start learning how to play the drums which is beyond this short introduction to drumming. Check out the Time Space and Drums exercise book series available on Amazon US or Amazon UK.

However, I have included some bass drum exercises to help you on your way. And again, regarding tempo - Start at 60 bpm and speed up only when you are ready as previously stated.

Create a practice routine based around the bass drum exercises and then practice the bass drum for a couple of weeks or months. It should go without saying but practice the rudiments with your feet too to get them working.

After following the hands and feet position tips in the Time and Space Part One & Two exercise books you should practice the bass drum using ¼ notes, $1/8^{th}$ notes, $1/16^{th}$ notes, and triplets for a full four bars each then play them all together for four bars of each consisting of 1 bar ¼ notes, 1 bar $1/8^{th}$ notes, one bar $1/16^{th}$ notes then 1 bar of triplets and then repeat the whole exercise. Again, build the bass drum skill up over a period of weeks and months. Then add the Hi-Hat Pedal playing the quarter note (1, 2, 3, and 4) then again playing $1/8^{th}$ notes on the hi-hat. This is just to get your feet working singularly as well as together.

ADD HI-HAT Pedal left Foot

Adding the hi-hat pedal will help develop the bass drum Right Foot, Hi-Hat Left Foot, and the coordination between the two. You should develop these two using the previously mentioned bass drum exercise daily for a few weeks to increase your ability and coordination.

Here you will become acutely aware of the concept of balance between the two feet, legs, and whole body which is a very important aspect of drumming.

The goals discussed above have been all about practice and development and should be adhered to conscientiously throughout your drumming career. Improvement is the name of the game, improvement of yourself, and of your drumming - your drumming abilities will be a direct reflection of yourself development and your state of mind and being. We should all strive to improve our skills and ourselves as no-one is perfect, but perfection is and always is a long-term goal or desired outcome. Knowing you will never get there is the whole point of striving to get there. We, humans, love a challenge!

We become masterful in the process, so again let's travel a little further down the road to drumming mastery.

In the free drumming booklet/sales letter titled: **In the Beginning - Creating a Universe** available through Time Space and Drums Peart 1, that I wrote in the 90's displays the importance of all of this stuff, how to think about it and travel down the road to drumming mastery with a pre-prepared plan or vision of the actions that need practicing and integrating into your playing. You really will get out what you put in.

TASK: The task here is simply to "begin practicing the fundamentals slowly and build accuracy and speed over time". There is no rush.

Note that the more you practice these fundamentals the more "Technique" comes into what you play and how you play it. But again, the noise of long practice sessions can as previously mentioned be a problem.

TURN THOSE DRUMS DOWN!

As with anything in life, concentrating on the problem will only make the problem seem bigger and will go nowhere to actually solving the problem. To solve the problem of noise we have to take steps like the ones previously mentioned until we find ourselves able to solve the problem altogether or make adaptations to our development practice.

Here we are going to presume that our problem exists and persists.

THE LAST RESORT or Is It?

Something I touched on earlier recently came to my attention and after serious contemplation, I discovered that this solution to the noise problem supplies us with a fantastic opportunity for growth both personally and as drummers.

AIR PLAYING

What! Air playing? you have to be kidding right? No, not kidding. Air Playing is a fantastic way to develop your drumming knowledge, understanding, and actual skills.

A lot of people learn by playing the air or "Air Playing". They literally pretend there is a drum kit in front of them but at first glance, this may seem crazy, even insane but if we take a closer look at what we have touched upon already in this short book, adding visualizations to your air playing is a very powerful way to improved understanding and skill on the drum kit.

This concept can even be helpful to advanced drummers. Advanced drummers and teachers are just students on a different journey and at a different point in their own journey. Advanced drumming is simply the mastery of the basic concepts and the further development of those basic concepts, but back to the point.

What is really happening when we "air play" is working on two different levels.

1. You are bringing the mind into perfect alignment with the body to a degree based on the mind's understanding of a concept.

2. Controlling what you are doing now and what you are going to do next in order to bring into being a better result.

SUBCONSCIOUS IGNORANCE

The subconscious mind doesn't know the difference between a pretended act of visualizing a particular performance and an actual performance. It has been proven that the subconscious is totally ignorant and therefore the same degree of enthusiasm during the rehearsed performance as well as the effects of such a performance would be produced such as sweating, getting stiff and tired, etc. It is as though you actually finished playing a gig with your favorite band.

He who understands (via visualization techniques taken from drumming theory) becomes a much greater drummer than he who doesn't for the simple reason that his whole being including his subconscious mind is on board, supporting the performance and practice. His practice becomes internalized and he gets clearly defined images of the concepts involved in his drumming and the results that he gets.

This is why music theory is so vital to the mental picture but all too often overlooked in favor of the fun stuff.

Trust me playing great whether what your playing is simple or difficult is much more fun.

The Theory of Practice - The Theory behind the Theory - 4 Stages of Learning.

To demonstrate, there is a simple system that clearly shows all of what we have been talking about here and so I would like to illustrate it using this simple formula. There are four stages in this process and it's a process we all go through when knowingly or not within every subject material. But here we are speaking metaphorically of drumming and out personal abilities. The stages are:

1. **You do not know what you don't know.** *(You don't know what you need to know to improve at anything).* It is unconscious or unknown to you.

2. **You know what you don't know.** - *(You have learned and therefore now know what it is that was holding you back. You're aware of the solution).* You are consciously aware.

3. **You Know What You Know.** - *(You have practiced and therefore now know what it was that you didn't know before but now do through experiencing or practicing it).* Constant conscious effort or practice.

4. **You know that you know.** - *(You have practiced and have perfected the exercises and are now able to teach them to others – you play them automatically).* It has become unconscious again or automatic.

In stage 4 above you have become the teacher. but it is vital that at step 4 there are still other things that you don't know, and on, and on, and on and on the cycle goes.

In other words. You are always learning, or should be. Please reread the four stages to make sure that you completely understand the process before you move on.

"Constant Never-Ending Improvement" makes the master of drums the student, and the student the master, for everyone as something they can teach even if it's what not to do? And everyone has something new to learn.

I call this: **from the beginning to the end and back.** It's a constant cycle or journey!

PLAYING DRUMS IS EASY

From the standpoint of the previous chapters of this little book, it's clear to see that "Learning to play the drums Is easy". It only becomes difficult if you want to play exercise 56 when you haven't perfected exercise 1 yet. Even exercises 2, 3, or 4 will be difficult if you haven't perfected exercise 1. That is the way I designed the Time Space and Drums Series. It's a step-by-step progressive development program in learning how to play the drums.

What do I mean by perfect?

When I say perfect I really mean internalized as demonstrated in the previous 4 stages of learning, I could count you in and you're instantly able to play the exercise from the written example or from memory. It is internalized.

So, by using a simple step by step approach method just about everything we learn becomes easy. Here are the steps to learning something:

1. Get to know the exercise (through seeing it written down in musical form and hearing it played). Thereby understanding it mathematically, theoretically, or scientifically.

2. Practice the simple exercise. Learn the movements involved to produce the practice material.

3. You perfect the simple exercise. After constant, conscious practice and effort. (refer to the above 4 steps or stages of learning in particular stage 3).

At which stage you don't know the next step - until you do, right? Then you practice that and perfect that and the process continues and repeats.

That is the process to learn to play drums or anything else. If you're impatient then you may struggle with exercise 1 simply because you have exercise 40 on your mind. This is also the cause of overwhelm.

This is why the visualizing method works so well, it not only brings your mind into sync with your playing, but it also brings the playing into sync with your mind so that both can work integrally towards drumming mastery.

WHEN IS THE BEST TIME TO BEGIN LEARNING DRUMS?

From the moment we are born we begin learning. A baby learns to sit, and then stand, then walk then asks its parents for more pocket money - well you get the picture.

It's a step by step approach. Learning anything is a step by step approach and therefore simple. We just need to discipline ourselves to focus on the step we are learning at any particular time to eliminate the chance of becoming overwhelmed.

What we learn and at what age we are when we learn it is an unimportant factor. It is the application and effort we expend which is important. So, whether you are 4 or 40, 40 or 60 it is the perfect time to learn. If you can hold the drumsticks you can learn to play the drums.

If you are going def though watch out for the neighbors knocking?

A COMMON MISCONCEPTION

As I have mentioned the brain forms "new neural pathways" when we learn anything. When we learn more about a particular subject the neural pathways become deeper and more ingrained into our memories and the newer neural pathways are created. Just like the branches of a tree and the fact that the branches are thickest at the root and thinner at the ends where more new neural pathways need building first to further that particular branch of the tree, our brains and the area or branch of knowledge we are studying.

Knowing this gives us a clear picture and tells us that as drummers we do not divide our limbs to be able to play different things at different times within a drum beat but that we are all the time heading towards integrating the limbs - this is akin to an airplane heading for a certain destination thousands of miles away. Hundreds of tiny course corrections have to be made in order to safely arrive at the destination.

Concentrating on the right foot on the bass drum is akin to a course correction. Many integrated course corrections lead to the final destination safely.

The limbs are brought together into sync and we discover that before we practiced a particular drumbeat, they were divided, but working integrally in the everyday tasks of walking, running, making breakfast, etc. because we have already learned those actions or movements.

In respect to walking, the legs are integrated and working together in order for a certain result to occur - arrival at a certain point - or cooperating with each other.

It is the perception of a student that a good guide changes in order to get the best results out of the student drummer. Who then travels the road to become master of time space and drums.

So, Now Let's Talk About Me

That heading is a little vain I know, but in this instance necessary. I am not, never was, and never will be the greatest drummer in the world or even close. So, why is that? It's very simple, although I love drums, both playing them and writing about them... It's just not in me. I mean, I am not made that way.

I used to practice a heck of a lot, sometimes 10 hours per day. In fact, whilst many other drummers were gigging, I was practicing and so I wondered for many years why I wasn't one of the great drummers. The answer to that question eluded me for a long time until one day I discovered a book by a fellow called Jay Niblick titled: What's Your Genius? Let me give a brief overview of that books' contents.

In it, Jay talks about authenticity being the prime quality in the results and success level of someone's life. So, you could say that the most successful people are the ones being authentic to their natural talents, but what does that mean? Simply put, we are all born with something like (and these are just example numbers as I forget the actual number involved, but these numbers serve our purpose here) Six hundred billion neural pathways in our brains but most of those pathways die by the time we reach 6 months old. We are then left with a measly six billion neural pathways.

The point then is that we are all left with different pathways that give us unique abilities. I would highly recommend that you get the book for yourself and take the D.I.S.C Test that goes along with the book. It's basically an assessment of your natural talents and it is very fascinating. There are various tools that help you discover your strengths and talents but I found this to be the best, backed up with more research, and also produced better results. Those results being based on results that I actually understood to draw an accurate picture of myself and how I had moved through life up to that point.

The book's subtitle "How the Best Think for Success" gives an insight into the contents of the book. It deals with how you look at yourself and if accepted helps you move through life in a more authentic way. But we are talking about drumming here so look at it this way, the book will help you get the most out of your natural talents whatever they may be.

For example, you may discover that you have specific talents and skills that you can adapt to your drumming and goals to get the most from your natural talents and from your drumming as well as life in general.

Now let's get back to me. Just kidding, I discovered that my particular talent was presentations, which made complete sense to me for a few reasons. The main one being that although I wasn't the best when it came to technique and technical ability on the drums, I did sort of play beyond those inadequacies. What I mean by that is that if I were put in a practice room with a master technician, he could blow me away as they say. But when it came to playing an actual performance, I discovered that I geared everything towards that performance.

So, when I *presented* myself on stage to play a gig whether it was with a local club entertainer in my early days or a major celebrity playing on one of my most recent gigs I would sort of stop, and present myself.

Actually, I presented the drumming in most cases with exactly what was needed for that particular gig. I didn't need to be a technician. I had practiced what I needed to in order to get where I wanted to get. In short, it was all about the *presentation* for me but the presentation of the drumming to the music and in a way that injected the right amount of energy and skill for a particular gig or show.

In a way, I am doing the exact same thing now. I am or will be presenting the Time Space & Drums series to you the drummer and if I look at it like that it makes me want to work on the designs of the books, the images associated with the books and all of the writing behind the books in my goal of presenting something of unique value to you. The more I focus on the presentation of the values that I hope will serve you best interests the more I will succeed in my endeavors.

I say this simply to illustrate that my own strengths even though may not be directly related to playing the drums they serve me in that they allow me to present something of value for you. Therefore, when you learn your true talents and strengths this may help you find a way to take advantage of those strengths and apply them to your drumming and life.

I was never great at practicing with bands in my early day because consciously and subconsciously I was learning so that when it came to the crunch, I played the drums, I played the music. I presented my abilities really well because my natural talents and authenticity came into play when I got on the stage or into the pits of a large theatre.

Intermediate Drummer Tips

This is all moving into really quite advanced stuff about the drummer and not just the drumming which makes perfect sense to me as sometimes we have to check the oil before the car runs at its optimum and in the same way we have to check ourselves before we get the most out of our abilities. It also makes these basic concepts covered here suitable for beginning drummers as well as intermediate and even advanced players. Finding our natural talents and authenticity is more about the drummer than playing the drums. That said, up until this section of the book most of the techniques and tips were aimed at the beginner who was starting from scratch without a drum kit.

Then when we spoke about understanding we sort of developed into intermediate drummer territory where it was important to understand what we were playing and that development of the inner sight of the drummer was just as important if not more so than the external playing of the drums. Even though we are not focusing on the inner workings as we play, practice and development doesn't mean that nothing is occurring within ourselves. To a great extent, our inner life is reflected and also influences our outer life.

This is demonstrated when you see some drummers or perhaps you have done it yourself at some time, they look up into the air. Well, they are not actually looking up into the air at all, they are looking up to hopefully find an inner picture of the concept of drumming they are playing at that time and that would help them play better or keep the great playing up by controlling it.

From an external point of view, it looks as if they look up as if to better help their concentration but searching for that image in the mind of the concepts, they need at a particular time is helping their concentration. Well, it would if they had easy recall of the images in mind and not just staring up into blank space and hoping for something to happen?

Some people look down and others look to the side but they are actually just trying to gain a better concentration on what they are doing at the time through the images in their mind.

You will notice this in general in yourself. If for instance, someone asks you a question in 90% of cases you will immediately look within and start scanning your inner mind looking for the solution or answer to the question being asked.

Dave Weckl calls this same thing, or similar at least, "listing to yourself as if you were listening to another drummer as if you were listening to yourself from a tape recorder." Please see The Nest Step video.

When you look at both ideas what Dave is really saying is that he projects himself, rather he projects his consciousness outside of himself and visualizes himself playing the drums on a tape recorder but more concerned with the sound than the actual image of himself playing the drums. The visualization of him playing would be most likely subconscious to the conscious act of listening to the music as a whole in order to be able to visualize the drums in a way that gave him access to… listening to the volume of each drum and the time playing etc.

So, we see that even the greats master this technique in one form or another. You could also say that when Dave talks about "singing what you play" he is internalizing a particular rhythm and singing it or he is visualizing and singing. He has a complete understanding of the notes, rhythms, and sounds that he sings. In that, there has to be some form of visualization involved whether conscious or unconscious, visual or auditory. All the great athletes use it so why wouldn't all the great drummers?

At an intermediate level of drumming ability, the development of the visual aspect of music is quite essential due to the fact that consciousness is formed of concepts which are visualized nuggets of truths that we learn as we move onto more advanced techniques.

Advanced Techniques

The book Advanced techniques for the modern drummer is brought to mind as I wrote that title section "Advanced Techniques". You see to me because I was never a really great technician or there was a point, I didn't go beyond in my playing… all of the advanced techniques are only advanced from the none drummer, beginner drummer and intermediate drummers' point of view.

If you are learning anything in a step-by-step process or manner and mastering the exercises as you go, most drumming becomes quite easy although that "easy" may take many forms and contain many levels of "easy". Especially when the music and coordination required becomes really complex, or indeed easy depending on your perspective.

This is why the four stages or levels of learning is such a useful tool. It tells you where you are and where you need to go. To illustrate, let's rewrite those levels in a much simpler form and relate them to drumming.

Stage 1: You don't know what you need to learn and practice.

Stage 2: You know what you need to learn and practice.

Stage 3: You are now practicing what you need to learn and practice.

Stage 4: You have practiced what you needed to practice.

So, you see from the 4 stages that at stage 1 you simply don't know what needs to be learned and practiced. You are blind to what you need to learn in order to get better because you don't know the subjects involved well enough to know that you need to learn more in a particular direction. If you take reading music, for example, you don't know how to read music because you haven't purchased a music theory book to learn from. You may not have known that they even exist?

If you can't read music and you do have a music theory book then you know what you need to learn and practice. You're at stage 2.

If you are now already learning from a music theory book then you are at stage 3 and on the journey towards stage 4. Only when you have learned, studied, and practiced the techniques from the music theory book will you reach stage 4.

All four stages are part of a larger journey I like to call "From the beginning to the end and back". That constant cycle of learning and practicing takes us from ignorance to mastery then back to ignorance. The time you spend in a state of ignorance is dependent on your ability to gain information and act on that information until you become a master of the information subject matter. But remember when we used the cold and hot water analogy? You never are really ignorant and you are never really the master. Instead, you simply are, just like Shakespeare and his "to be or not to be".

Simply put, wherever you find yourself within a certain subject matter you now know what needs to be done to become the master of that subject.

Put another way the 4 stages of learning imply certain things to us.

Stage 1: Implies setting goals for ourselves. Seeking out answers to questions we ask ourselves but, in many cases, never actually seek or ask the questions.

Stage 2: Implies scheduling our goals. Making plans to reach a now known end or result.

Stage 3: Implies attitude. Or the way that you play what you play. This is the action stage where you perform the tasks required to reach your goals. This is often the place people get stuck because they didn't take care of stages 1 and 2?

Stage 4: Implies that we need to relearn or seek out more ways to improve what we already know which takes us back to stage 1 and beyond.

Throughout the process and processes that we go through to become better drummers or better at anything on our way to mastery, we are really grinding the neural pathways in our brains deeper and deeper so that the subject matter is more easily available to us when we invoke them from memory which again in itself is a process of visualizing that which we are learning or practicing.

Memory itself is an act visualization. We go through stage 3 until the memory is more easily recallable and we reach stage 4 when we recall the memory automatically and instantly at will.

Advanced techniques are the basic fundamentals played masterfully. - Stephen Hawkins

That quote I wrote some time ago is true from my own personal perspective but it may not be true for you, especially if you are a more advanced drummer. That quote may need expanding on if you are an advanced player but which way do you expand it? In truth, you don't.

What? "That makes no sense", I hear you say. You would be right it **does** make absolutely no sense whatsoever. But it also makes perfect sense. What I mean to say is that it makes perfect sense from your perspective simply because what you the more advanced drummer sees as a basic fundamental is an advanced technique from the perspective of a complete beginner or even intermediate drummer.

It really isn't a case of who is right and who is wrong in anything, it is merely a different perspective that divides people, that makes them unique.

Where you are on the journey to drumming mastery will determine your perspective, therefore:

1. What goals you set for yourself (in drumming and life).
2. What your schedule looks like.
3. What you need to do to improve your attitude and/or technique.
4. How you manage being the master and more easily able to step into the student's shoes.

I keep reflecting on Dave Weckl's Back to Basics video and how he blew us all away with his stick technique and drummers around the world were practicing their finger technique like crazy.

Then later in the Evolution videos, he had completely changed how he was playing. He had incorporated various other techniques and integrated them with the Back to Basics techniques. If you examine that little inconsistency you would realize that as Dave Weckl was the master of the Back to Basics Techniques, he was most likely unconscious to the Evolution techniques? He was at stage 4 with Back to Basics and stage 1 with the Evolution videos. But then reached stage 4 in the Evolution videos too.

This is all just an observation from my point of view and indeed Dave could have planned it all out ahead but this does serve as a good illustration of the learning and development process and that at some time or another Dave Weckl would have been at stage 1 in everything that he did or didn't know? You get the picture.

What You Play and Where You Play It.

So, we know the process of learning what to play which is really an evolution from one exercise to the next given to you by a teacher or guide in a step-by-step manner. So now let's touch on a subject that is really far too deep to go into but I thought it deserved a mention. TIME, but before we do let's take a look at space.

Space is the drummers' playground, it's where you play what you actually play. Let us presume then that you are playing 4 quarter notes (crotchets) in a repetitive manner in 4/4 time on the hi-hats. This technique accents the importance of air playing as well as practicing on a cushion that we mentioned earlier and remember that *advanced techniques are basic fundamentals played masterfully?* and this is a perfect example of that quote actualized.

You see, the whole point of practicing on a cushion isn't to play great drums. Apart from being helpful in solving a noise issue with family and neighbors, it's to play great space. In other words, to learn the movements of the arms, the flow. The Pulse. Now let's dig deeper.

Time Does Not Exist

That's right I said it, time does not exist. From the drummer's perspective if you play those 4 notes we mentioned above, then rested your stick on the hi-hat cymbals and let it rest there and stilled yourself blocking all around you out completely. Stillness is all there is or more aptly space is all there is. That space is your greatest tool as a drummer.

Time passes only for the external world which you just blocked out mainly because they are all acting on an external time measuring device, a clock. All you have is stillness or space as we just said. Now from that point, if you lift your stick off of the hi-hat cymbals and to the highest point of your striking distance then moved your arm, hand, wrist, and fingers down toward the hi-hat cymbals a second time… well, you just created time. If you repeat that motion you create more time and with every movement, you create more and more time, within the space available.

You see time is created by movement. Without movement, the time couldn't exist. And hence the better you play that movement the better you sound when you hit those hi-hat cymbals with the tip or shoulder of your stick.

Whether you use the tip or the shoulder of the stick is determined by the type of music you are playing, your conscious decision to hit the hi-hat cymbals in that particular place, the amount of time you take to hit the cymbals again, and the force used to bring the stick up and down onto those cymbals. In other words, the combined techniques used or the movements you make in creating said time or hitting the hi-hat.

In summation to that description, I would like to say, "Dave Weckl isn't a great drummer *(let me finished, no-one ever said those words together in a full sentence before now – I'm getting a little dizzy just hearing them for the first time strung together in that order)* … he isn't a great drummer because he plays great drums. I am saying that Dave Weckl plays the drums great because he is a great drummer?

Do you see the difference? The drummer came first, then the drums were mastered. Of course, the two aspects integrate but the drummer always comes first.

To become masterful, you need to be masterful. Every tap of a drum, every nuance, every movement should be masterfully performed in order to make the hi-hat sound masterful. The master must come before the masterful playing? And unfortunately, or perhaps fortunately for most of us, the student must come before the master.

So again, we see that perspective comes into play. Who you perceive you are will determine who you become? You cannot become something you don't see yourself as being?

Many books have been written on the subject of self-image so I won't go too deep into it here but how you see and perceive yourself is of paramount importance, but remember arrogance is not attractive. I believe the best book on the subject is Psycho-Cybernetics by Maxwell Maltz, he was a plastic surgeon who also helped people solve their self-image problems' often through surgery.

Have you ever heard this question before? To be or not to be, that is the question?

Well of course you have and so be. Simply that, be who you want to become/be. And you will one day become it in every moment of now.

Changing the subject slightly I would highly recommend another book by Seth Godin titled: The Dip. It is really about assessing yourself and knowing when quitting is a good thing, but beyond that, he gives some great insights into winning at anything and the process of winning which can serve anyone's life for the better when you are aware of it *(notice that this implies that you may be at stage 1 in knowing the subject matter of this book)* whatever you decide to do with your life. However, the book makes great mention of the stage three process and why most people don't make the GOAT (greatest of all time) list.

Measuring Time

If time is a movement then how do we measure it? Well although quite an advanced concept time is easily measurable.

If you yourself count the song off (or in) then you decide the measurements but if a band leader counts you in then the measurement is external and so some external focus will be required on your part.

Once you have the pulse then you have the spaces. The spaces remember, determine your movements needed in order to be "on time" with the external or internal count off or pulse. So, we see the importance of preparation through either tapping the foot or watching someone else's foot as well as hand movements in order to start off on time with the rest of the band or indeed alone yet on time if you are practicing.

It's also a good idea to interpret an external or internal source of time with some action of your own to let other members of the band know what pulse you are getting and to help internalize the external time source. This will give the other members of the band a better idea as to what the pulse is going to be when the count begins.

After these preparations are made and you are playing the music we move into the internal territory of your own mind. That is, presuming that you are not reading a drum chart. At which time, you would still be focusing on the pulse mostly within and on an unconscious level at this point along with the actual written music.

So, now presuming that the music is moving along how do we measure the time. Simple, by visualizing it.

Imagine if you will a point at the back of your neck. From that point draw an imaginary circle within your mind starting at the back of your neck, going over and above your head and beyond over the front of your face down through your heart area and back to the point at the back of your neck. This circle should be approximately 6-8 feet in diameter. It is, of course, a transparent imaginary circle which should now encompass the other members of a small band. Or if you are practicing a straight-ahead rock beat then it will include no one else but you.

The point here is that if you look at the circle from the side and divide the circle into 4… top, right, bottom, left, and top again. You see the 12 o'clock, 3 o'clock, 6 o'clock and 9 o'clock position markers, or the quarter notes. Then divide the circle again into 8th notes and again into 16th notes and then again into 32nd notes.

Put another way, divide the circle into 4 quarters. Then divide each quarter into halves. Then divide each quarter into eight.

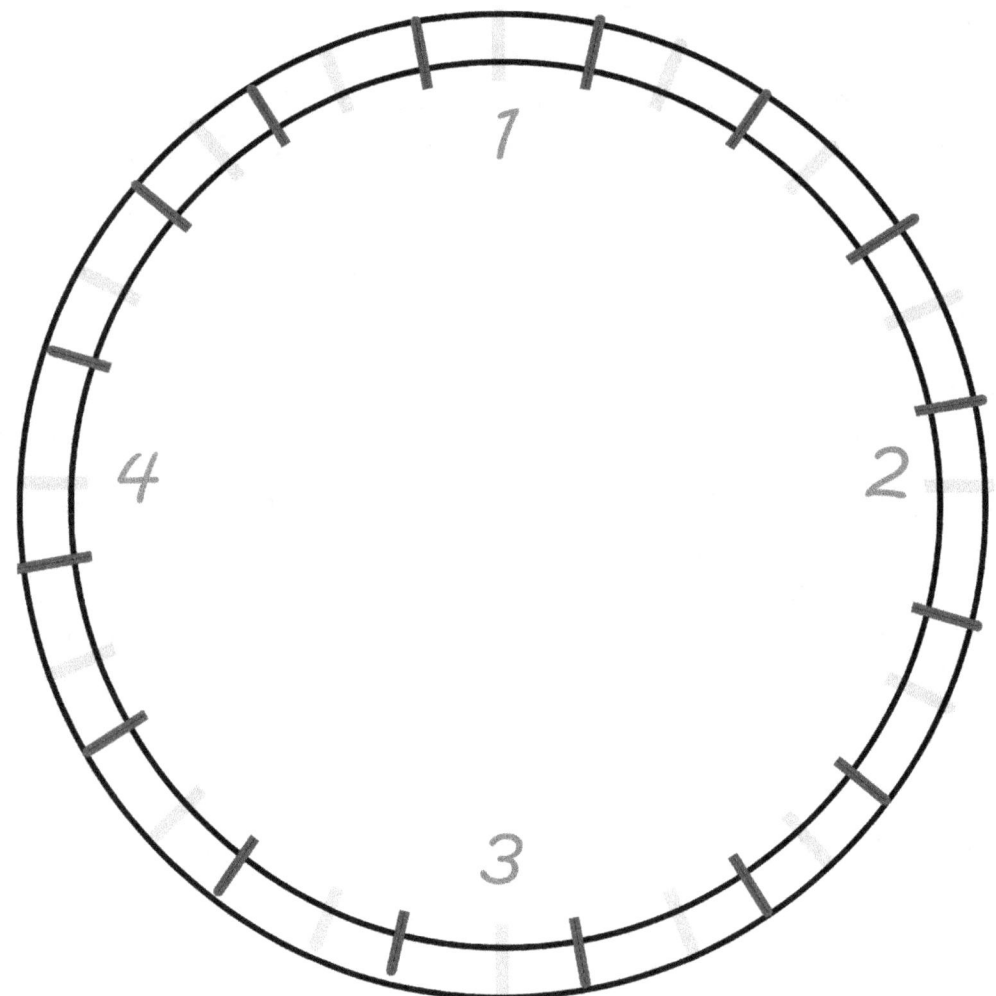

The above sketch shows the kind of thing I mean. However, bear in mind that this is not a solid structure. It is transparent and movable.

The time we create is much like Bruce Lee's analogy of water. He said something akin to, "movements should be slow and fluid, much like water, when you pour water into a cup the water becomes the cup. Be the water, be the cup".

As a drummer, be the time, be the song or music that you play, which in turn implies getting to know the song or music piece intimately in a theoretical, musical notation, and mathematical manner. In the end, this is why music theory is so important. So, you can bend to the flow of the music despite how complex it becomes?

The above analogy should serve as an idea as to what I am getting at. Flow through it *(the circle, the time, the music)* in a fluid yet measured way then your playing will begin to flow much as Bruce Lee describes. You become the time and music.

The Point

The point of this visualization exercise is to not constantly view this circle in your mind. First, it is to get you to see that the notes themselves, the ones that are "on-the-beat" are very much smaller than the space it takes to hit or play a particular note. Or, the spaces in-between the notes are very much larger than the notes themselves and so this allows more time to concentrate on your arm and hand movements until you hit each note perfectly on time.

And second, you begin to see time as a solid controllable concept that you yourself control. Space and Time are your most powerful tools apart from yourself and your drums of course.

So, the idea is to get you to look into that space, and instead of focusing on, let's say 4 quarter notes. Instead, focus on the space or the measurements between the notes, and that makes up a particular note. It is your inner microcosm or universe, with time flowing in a never-ending circle in a fluid motion all the time-bending to the surrounding music.

You can quite easily change the circle into a flat line and have the measurements run along that line much like actual notes would appear on the staff and then visualize the measurements or spaces either as actual musical notes or measurements. You could also visualize time as a square instead of a circle, the choice is yours.

Those spaces are then made up of your arm movement which is made in a smooth flowing fashion much like the cushion exercise from earlier and much like Bruce Lee describes the water and cup exercise.

Original Title

When I first created the Time Space and Drums Series, I was originally going to create videos and a whole program for learning how to play the drums. But it struck me that behind my thinking wasn't a set of ideas that would make myself look great as a drummer but instead to allow the student to concentrate or learn what could make them great.

The original title was: DRUMMING: The Art and Science of Time & Space because that is exactly what drumming is all about. Hence space and universe theme that runs throughout the series in the titles of the individual books themselves.

It then struck me that in reality most of what we do as drummers is to mold the space into time through the movements we make.

This idea itself implies an art form, which it is but behind that artform is the science. Whilst the old title suggests time and space, the Time Space and Drums Series is really about the science, or the movements that you make and not how you make those movements. That is why the series is very exercise-oriented and those exercises are laid out in a step-by-step fashion which implies the creation of something. In this case, the creation of your own universe of drumming skills and abilities. Your own time and your own space.

Beyond this basic concept, we move into the territory of drumming technique which is beyond the scope of this little book and the Time Space and Drums Series.

For now, I will leave you with a single quote I developed as the Time Space and Drums Series developed, from its beginnings until now.

"Master the art of leaving space, then the things you play in time become great"

- *Stephen Hawkins*

I wish you every success on your journey.

Closing Note:

The Time Space and Drums series is intended as a complete program from Part 1 to Part 12 plus this supplemental concept book. Should you decide to follow the Time Space and Drums series it is strongly advised that you follow the program in order of the individual series parts as they integrate and build on each other.

The only thing I can now add is that you should practice each exercise within the series until you have them all mastered. Mastery comes from paying attention to the most basic fundamentals already covered in each of the exercises within the series.

Once you have perfected each exercise you may like to try them left-handed but that may take time depending on your current skill level.

Afterword

Thank you for choosing Time Space and Drums as one of your learning tools. I hope you enjoyed this book and continue to enjoy the process of improving your drumming through the whole series. You can explore more of the series as the Time Space and Drums series parts become available from your favorite book store.

Want to stay up to date with news about my books?

* Like me on Facebook: Facebook.com/TimeSpaceAndDrums

* Follow me on Twitter: Twitter.com/TimeSpaceDrums

Finally, don't forget to join the Time Space and Drums Community where you can meet, chat, and share your drumming videos and experiences with other Time Space and Drums members.

Thank you again and I hope we meet again between the pages of another book. Remember, You rock!

Did You Enjoy Reading This Time Space and Drums Book?

I would like to thank you for purchasing and reading this book. I hope you enjoyed it and that it provided some value to yourself, your life, and your drumming.

If you enjoyed reading this book and found some benefit in it, I'd love your support and hope that you could take a moment to post a review. Any feedback, will help me in ensuring that I improve this book and others in the future.

Click Here To Leave Your Review

https://www.amazon.com/dp/1913929124

Other Books by The Author

Modern Drumming Concepts (Supplemental to the Time Space and Drums Series)
Rock Drumming Foundation Course. (Six in-depth Drum Lessons).
Jazz Drumming Foundation Course. (Six in-depth Drum Lessons).
Rock Drumming Development Course. (Six in-depth Drum Lessons).
Jazz Drumming Development Course. (Six in-depth Drum Lessons).
Odd Time Drumming Foundation Course. (Six in-depth Drum Lessons).
Music Minus Drummer Collection. (Six in-depth Drum Lessons).
Accents and Phrasing Course. (Four in-depth Drum Lessons).
Basic Latin Drumming Foundation Course. (Four in-depth Drum Lessons).
Developing Creativity Volume 1. (Four in-depth Drum Lessons).
Developing Creativity Volume 2. (Four in-depth Drum Lessons).
Developing Creativity Volume 3. (Five in-depth Drum Lessons).
Developing Creativity Volume 4. (Six in-depth Drum Lessons).

www.ingramcontent.com/pod-product-compliance
Lightning Source LLC
Chambersburg PA
CBHW081355080526
44588CB00016B/2507